RED V...
and t...
LUBIA...

by

Raphael Rupert

as edited by

Hugh W. L. Weir

BALLINAKELLA *Paperbacks*
Whitegate, Co. Clare, Ireland.

© 1991
Dr. Raphael Rupert and Ballinakella *Paperbacks*
(This Edition, Equally).

This Edition published by Ballinakella *Paperbacks,*
Whitegate, Co. Clare, Ireland in 1991.
All rights reserved.

British Library Cataloguing in Publication data.
A catalogue record for this book is available from the
British Library.

ISBN 0 946538 09 3

Author: Raphael Rupert.

Editor: Hugh W. L. Weir.

General layout and advice: Grania Weir, Tomás Porcell.

Cover: Hugh W. L. Weir.

Type Input: Grania Weir, Helen Cronin.

Type setting: Tomás Porcell.

Printing: Colour Books Limited.

INTRODUCTION

This is a true story. Dr. Raphael Rupert experienced one of the most devastating twentieth century inhumanities, and yet he has written a factual and fascinating account of his treatment in Soviet concentration camps and even at the hands of his own people. Although, as Edward Crankshaw wrote in his introduction to the "Hidden World" *, the previous edition of his story, Raphael Rupert "had already had glimpses of Soviet reality under Stalin, he had no clear picture of what he would have to suffer and when he was finally sentenced to twenty-five years forced labour, on a trumped-up charge of espionage for the British, he went off on that appalling prison train as on a voyage of discovery". He viewed his circumstances from his own specific standpoint but this was so firm that he took it completely for granted. It was that of the convinced instinctive liberal individualist. The son of a distinguished Hungarian liberal politician, Dr. Rupert answered what he believed to be his call to duty by helping allied airman and Jews escape from the Nazis. This was the most natural and liberal thing for him to do. His liberalism was simply the principle of freedom to be oneself; something which he was himself to be so cruelly denied.

Amongst the final pages of "Red Wire and the Lubianka," Dr. Rupert takes us into the world of prison camps as they are in the process of being broken up and gives us an insight as to the Soviet way of doing things, even when the intentions are good rather than evil. The fascinating record of his final interrogations in the Lubianka prison, as a witness for the prosecution of Beria's accomplices rather than as an accused, gives us a unique insight, from behind the scenes, of the "agonised process of de-stalinisation as it affected the apparatus of police terror". In the earlier pages of the book, the reader is simply given a day to day, eight year long, account of what happened to an unassuming Central European caught up in "the insane ferocity of ideological warfare", including his arrest in Budapest in 1947, his violent treatment at the hands of his own countrymen, his imprisonment and interrogation which ended in a false confession and his sentence, and the horrifying and macabre account of his long train journey to Russia and the concentration camps. Dr. Rupert's insights into aspects of Soviet life, especially in remote areas where it was even impossible to tell a free citizen from a prisoner, the swift sexual encounters, his touching comments on the Russian countryside, his appreciation of the clergy of different denominations and religions and his own efforts to make the best out of his circumstances, make fascinating reading.

To understand the mood behind Dr. Rupert's story, one should perhaps recall the "House of the Dead" by Dostoievsky, Gogol's "Dead Souls" or Chekhov's "Sakhalin Island" and realise that the same violence, the same squalor, venality, degradation and waste of human resources recorded in "Red Wire and the Lubianka" existed even before the Revolution. The "bandits" were the same in Dostoievsky's time, likewise the corruption.

Since the writing of this book, things have changed. But we must never forget the traumas and experiences of Dr. Rupert, his fellow prisoners and the many thousands of innocent people who have, through no fault of their own, been caught up in hideous and scary circumstances. It is their recollections which can contribute so much towards helping new genertions understand the futility of man's inhumanity to man and hopefully guide future leaders of the world towards a truly peaceful but just society for all.

Hugh Weir.

* *Collins, 1963*

To the memory of my
fellow prisoners.

ACKNOWLEDGEMENTS

Shortly after I escaped from Hungary in 1956, I taped my account of the previous nine years as a prisoner in Russia. A friend kindly typed it in Hungarian for me.

I would like to thank Miss Evelyn Pinching and Paul Ignotus who, among others, were responsible for translating my script into English, Mr. Anthony Rhodes who originally edited the story and Anne, my wife of the past thirty years. I would also like to acknowledge with thanks The Honourable Mrs. (Grania) Weir for undertaking the typing, Mrs. (Helen) Cronin who also contributed towards this task, Mr. Tomás Porcell for setting, layout and general design and Mr. Hugh Weir for editing "Red Wire and the Lubianka" and for the cover design.

Chapter 1

ARRESTED - June 1947

On 17th November, 1956, I landed at Blackbushe in England with the first batch of Hungarians to escape during the revolution.

A few days before, I had been persuaded to leave my country. I had only just been released after years of imprisonment in Russia and my friends were afraid that, if the rising collapsed, I might be given a further sentence on the suspicion that I had participated in it. Everything had happened so quickly that I had not even had time to change my clothes. I was still wearing my Russian prison uniform when I landed in Britain.

At the airfield my companions and I were met by various officials who took us to London and lodged us in a hotel. After a few days we were left to stand on our own feet and in the following months the British authorities made no attempt to cross-question us or to find out if we could give them useful information. This surprised me as, following my experiences in Russia, there was a lot of valuable stuff I could have told them. I discovered later, however, that this was the routine for dealing with political refugees. Security authorities preferred to leave them alone for some months (keeping them under observation) in case they approached, or were approached by, suspicious persons. Once they were convinced that an induvidual was a *bona fide* emigre, and would lead them to no espionage contacts, they would interview them.

After about seven months in England I was summoned to Whitehall. Although I had worked in an allied underground movement during the war, I was treated at first with suspicion and even hostility. Later, on reflection, I realised that all security forces are bound to adopt severe methods. At the time, however, I blurted out "Well, gentlemen, I can only tell you that you remind me of my Russion interrogators". Twelve years previously I had had my first experience of a Russian inquisition.

In summer, 1945 I had been sent for by some Russian officers in Budapest. They wanted to know why I would not cooperate with them politically, despite my interest in the Hungarian liberal party, and they also asked me about my wartime activities on behalf of the British. I consulted the British Military Mission in Budapest. They advised me to leave my country.

I was very reluctant to do this for I was anxious to reorganise the party of which my father had been a prominent member. My wife, also, who had a strong sense of family, said she would not leave "the tombs of my ancestors". However a second interrogation, far more disagreeable than the first, convinced me that I would be wise to cross to Austria. This I did in September.

While in Vienna, in order to live, I took a temporary job at the British Headquarters. A certificate from Field-Marshal Alexander in recognition of my wartime work helped me obtain this. Yet this minor administrative post as little more than a clerk was later to cause me to be shanghaied by the Russians, and to spend eight years in their concentration camps.

Months went by but things did not improve in Hungary. The leaders of the Hungarian "bourgeois" parties, my father among them, were gradually being supplanted, while the Communist nominees of the Russians became increasingly powerful. Undecided as to what to do, I applied for an immigration permit to Australia. There I hoped that, should the situation worsen, my wife might be prepared to start a new life with our children. Vienna was too close. When the permit was granted, I felt that I had to return to Budapest and discuss the matter with her, my father and the rest of my family. I decided that, as the Hungarian Communists would certainly not issue me a visa, I would have to enter the country illegally. Accordingly on the 4th June, 1947, I set off for the frontier with two friends who knew the crossing points.

I shall not forget that night as we crouched in the bushes near the border.

I had a desire to return to Vienna, a presentiment that something unpleasant would happen. One of my companions must have observed my fear, for he warned me to pull myself together and to keep an eye out for the guard dogs.

But the crossing turned out to be uneventful (in those days there were no minefields) and the following day, having taken the train from Gyor, I found myself back in Budapest.

Before going to my wife and father in the country, I decided to call on my brother-in-law in Budapest, and consult him. His advice was always sound. This was when I received my first shock. He refused to have me in the house. He would hardly speak to me, and even seemed frightened of me. It was the same with other friends I tried to see. "Are you mad to come back?" they demanded. "Don't you know what's happening here?"

At first no one would have me in their house, let alone offer me a bed. It was not until late in the evening that, after I had telephoned a number of friends, all of whom made polite excuses, that one of them saw my plight and took me in. That night in the doctor's flat was to be my last of freedom for nine years.

The next morning, as I was preparing to leave for the country, the front-door bell rang. I still must have had no real apprehension of danger, for I answered it myself, my friend having had already left on his rounds. I was confronted by a tall young man in civilian clothes who stated "I am a member of the security police. You must come with us for identification".

Outside on the steps, I saw another tough-looking young man who was holding a revolver. I was compelled to follow them. As I walked into the street, the full extent of the danger struck me and I cursed myself for having been so unperceptive. It took the actual physical appearance of the AVO men to make me appreciate my friend's warnings. I panicked and felt I must get away, at any cost. After silently accompanying these men for some minutes, I acted. The first was a little ahead of me, so I suddenly leapt at his colleague beside me and punched him hard on the jaw. He was unprepared for this and fell heavily. I turned and began running, while the other AVO man shouted to passers-by, "Catch him! He's a criminal!" He tried to grapple with me, but I also managed to knock him down. I began running as fast as I could, but people were gathering on both sides of the street, and I soon found myself surrounded by at least fifty people who blocked my escape on every side.

The first security man now ran up with a number of policemen who had mysteriously appeared from nowhere, I should have known that almost every third person in Budapest was now a representative of the police was again arrested, this time much less ceremoniously. I was bundled into a taxi with three policemen; the AVO man commanded the words "Andrassy Ut 60," and we set off for the security police headquarters. When we arrived, I was literally kicked out of the taxi by the two men I had struck. They pulled me inside and made me stand facing the wall, my hands above my head. "Shoot him if he moves!" they shouted.

I had to remain like this for nearly an hour. Whenever my arms tired and I lowered them, I was given a sharp blow in the ribs with a machine gun butt. Then the security man I had knocked down came in and began punching and kicking me. At length, covered with blood, I was taken upstairs to a large room in which, behind a desk, sat an officer in civilian clothes surrounded by more policemen. I was astounded, I saw it was my old friend Istvan Timar; we had been at the university together and I had later helped him with his studies when we had both been reading law. At the time, I was relieved to see him.

Timar glared at me. I received not a word of recognition or sympathy, nor a glance of compassion.

He suddenly barked, "Why did the British send you back to Budapest?"

By now I was really frightened. "The British?", I said. "Nobody brought me back. I came on my own. From Vienna. To see my family."

"We'll see about that," he said. "Are you the son of the Liberal politician?" He knew perfectly well, of course, who my father was, but he wanted to pretend that he had never had anything to do with me.

"Yes, I am," I said; adding that my father was now an old man, and that he had no intention of returning to politics.

"Why did you," Timar continued, "who once showed proper democratic tendencies, leave us? And not only did you leave us, but you went to Vienna to work for our enemies."

"Haven't you heard of my work for the British during the war, helping their escaped prisoners to get away from the Nazis?" I asked, "I did the same for the Jews. And for the Dutch. And for many Hungarians."

"That's true," he acknowledged. "You may have helped the Jews against Fascism once; we know that. But what have you been doing since? You've changed sides." He then began shouting again. "What were your contacts with the British in Vienna? Why did you go there? What was your job? You're a spy! Who gave you orders to organise spying in Hungary?"

I repeated that I had no idea what he was talking about, that I had never had the slightest connection with espionage, and that my job at the British Military Mission had been a minor one.

"Well, we'll try something else then," he said. "Take this piece of paper, sit at that table, and write down the whole story of the time you spent with the British in Vienna. If you do that fully and frankly, you may be able to save your skin."

He left me with the paper and pen for what must have been nearly two hours, and I wrote as accurately as I could about my activities in Vienna with the British. When he returned, he scornfully perused the three or four pages. "Take him out!" he said to the guards. "We'll give him twenty-four hours to think it over. Then perhaps he'll talk."

I was taken into another room without windows,

and which was lit by an extremely strong lamp. Here they made me stand against a wall while they searched my pockets. I was roughly undressed, receiving a number of blows on the head and in the stomach, one of which caused me such a sharp jabbing pain in the kidneys that I collapsed. I was then forced to hold my feet upwards so that they could beat the soles. Then the upper part of my feet and my ankles were whipped until they were swollen and bleeding.

I spent the night in this cell my only consolation being a loaf of bread and a blanket sent by my sister. The following day I was taken back for further interrogation. My ex-lawyer friend had now been replaced by a senior officer whom everyone addressed as "colonel". I wasto learnt later that before 1945, this "colonel" had been a municipal fireman. "We know that you belong to the British espionage service," he said. "Only by admitting the truth have you any chance of saving your life."

He questioned me about certain British and American organisations in Austria. I could, of course, give no proper answers to any of these questions, because I knew nothing about them. I had never heard of them.

"All right," he said, at length. "You're stubborn, I see. If you wont talk to us, perhaps you'd prefer to talk to the Russians. They'll be interested in you. You're a fool not to tell us the truth. Youll see what happens now. What you've just had is paradise compared with what you're in for."

Chapter 2

INTERROGATION - July 1947

The Russian major who now interrogated me had high cheekbones and slanting eyes. I had a feeling of having been handed over to Mongolians. Through an interpreter, he repeated the accusation that I had deserted to the greatest of their enemies, the British.

He then surprised me by mentioning the name of a British airman, Reginald Barratt, whom I had helped escape from Hungary during the war. In December 1944, I had helped Barratt cross to the Russian lines with special information which we had received secretly by radio from the West. My interrogator made the sinister observation that Reginald Barratt had really been a member of British Intelligence, and had been caught working in Russia as a double agent. He was now dead. In fact, he was not a double agent, but was nevertheless shot in Russia on 4th June, 1945. His name is inscribed on the R.A.F. War Memorial at Runnymede.

The interrogator continued by mentioning another old friend of mine, a Budapest dentist named Miklos Csomos who had also worked for the Underground during the war and knew Barratt. He said Csomos was now serving a life sentence in Russian for his hostility to the Russians.

"Do you want to end up the same way?", the major asked. "We believe you are one of the most dangerous members of the British military intelligence."

As the interrogation continued, he mentioned the names of further British and American officers and civilians working for the Allied headquarters in Vienna. He appeared to have the most detailed knowledge and was clearly anxious to impress me with the efficiency of the Russian security system. Having failed to obtain a "confession" he said irritably, "I must agree with your countrymen. You're very stubborn. But as your life depends on it, we'll give you plenty of time to think things over."

This was the first of a number of interrogations by this officer, in the course of which he mentioned the names of many of my Austrian friends, and of my relations who lived in Vienna. He referred to telephone calls I had made in that city, and told me their content. He read out conversations I had had, almost verbatim! I was astounded by his knowledge.

"We have time," he said at length. "We know all about you. We can afford to wait until you feel inclined to talk."

"If you know everything about me, then why go on interrogating me?" I asked. "Why keep me in this prison?"

During one interrogation, he made an offer which I half expected. Realising that he could still not obtain the "confession" he wanted, he suggested that I should work for the Russians, because my connections with the Western allies would make me very suitable for espionage work! I refused and the following day early in August 1947, I was handcuffed and taken by car to the Russian military headquarters at Baden, near Vienna.

It seems strange that Baden, this quiet watering place, in its setting of green fields and woods near Vienna, with its memories of Franz Joseph and his court, a typically

Hapsburg spa, should be the scene of my grimmest interrogation. But the Soviet High Command had chosen it as the Headquarters for their armies in Central Europe. It was now almost a Russian town.

I was interrogated nightly, in a much more leisurely but more thorough way, as if eternity lay before us. I must have repeated myself a hundred times in the next eight months. The Russians knew no Hungarian, and I no Russian, so the proceedings were conducted in German, which did not facilitate matters. Minutes of the proceedings were taken slowly, and for every question, which I answered in a few words, the interpreter would write for as long as an hour. The Russians, I discovered, are masters in the art of breaking down the morale of a prisoner. After what the Hungarian colonel had told me, I had imagined that they would physically torture me. But their method was to impose everlasting interrogations and dreary prison conditions, which at length induced a feelings of utter hopelessness and despair.

In my cell, as soon as I fell asleep at night, I would be shaken by guards and dragged upstairs to face the endless drumfire of the same old questions. Plain-clothed and uniformed officers would come in and whisper seriously to my interrogators, as if bringing special orders from higher quarters. They would look at me quizzically, as if I was some rare bird, and would sometimes ask me questions. Then, looking very wise, they would make copious notes.

Bright reflectors were sometimes turned on to my face, and four or five interrogators would mysteriously appear and place themselves in dark corners of the room, where I could not see them. I would then be attacked from all sides, the same questions being repeated as many as fifteen times in one night. Exhausted, I would be taken back to my damp cell. All was repeated the following night.

My interrogators were interested in everything and everybody I knew, down to the most remote school acquaintances whom I had not met for years. The manner in which they inquired about them was most ingenious. They knew that I was worried about my family, my friends and relations, and that I was frightened of involving them. They knew that I knew that anyone who had anything to do with me, a "British spy", might now be in danger. They therefore told me to speak of them openly, claiming that, anyway, they already knew all about them. Often the interrogator would mention a name casually, in passing from one subject to another and watch my reactions. He would say that they were simply trying to see if I was "decent", whether I told the truth or not.

The small hints about one's possible "decency", a kind of guarantee that they did not really want to harm one, gave the prisoner in solitary confinement a feeling that the interrogators were not necessarily his enemies. As they questioned me they smiled, that eternal smile, the Communist smile, calm, cynical, official. How well I was to get to know it in the next eight years!

"Old so-and-so, you haven't seen him for ten years, you say. Then," looking at me knowingly, "why did you draw him into your spy circle as a British agent?" I professed blank amazement, but they continued imperturbably. What were his tasks? When had he entered the British Service? Why did he, of all decent Hungarians, act against the progressive democratic countries?

Weeks passed, then months, in solitary confinement. Sometimes I was told that I would be confronted with a certain person I knew; tomorrow, the day after, next week; Rosen, Bauer, Csomos, or other officials I had known or heard of at the British Headquarters in Vienna. But the men with these names never came.

A less pleasant way of trying to persuade the prisoner to talk was to outline his future if he was "unco-operative". The lead and copper mines in Siberia and the coal mines in the Arctic tundra were described to me in detail. One of the interrogators spoke of life in the eternal snows and of gold mines of Kolyma in the Far East, of the hopelessness in the lumber camps thousands of miles from civilisation, of the exhausting labour on the new railway lines stretching out across the vast continent and of the lethal canal building. Finally the concentration camps where the prisoners lived were described.

They told me that there was no hope of escape from these camps. Their inhabitants would still be human beings in fifteen or twenty years' time, still alive to feel pain and hardship. How stupid the Germans had been to kill their prisoners! The Gestapo had foolishly tortured them so that they sometimes died! "Ridiculous!" my interrogator said. "We make our prisoners work. Why kill them? They can work until the last minute of their lives, all for us. When they cannot work any more, then they can die."

Such was life in Baden. It was worse for me than for the other prisoners, as I was not allowed out for exercise; I did not know when the sun was shining or the stars were out. As a British spy I was completely isolated.

In these months of loneliness I searched for any sign, or any trace of life which might keep me in contact with the world outside. I obtained a strange satisfaction from watching the spiders in the corners of their webs. I watched the flies come in through the iron grill, and thought, "How lucky they are! They're free! But how foolish to come in here, of all places!"

I watched the spider contemplating its prey in its independent little universe; the interminable fight of the fly for life, the victory of the strong over the weak. I saw the flies flying into the web and the astute spider first paralysing them with its sting, then ripping up the unsuspecting wanderer who had come in from the free world in search of something, to only find death. Was there not some similarity between my predicament and that of the fly?

Later, I discovered in one of the corners of the cell, an old chimney hatch that had been plastered over. The plaster was cracked and in one of the cracks I became aware of life; an animal was trying to get out. I watched for days, hoping this time not for insect, but for animal company. At last my patience was rewarded. A tiny pointed nose appeared in the crack; then I saw two sparkling little black eyes and two erect ears. A mouse came out and stared curiously around the cellar, as if looking for something. It approached me, even glanced up at me. Then it sat up on its two hind legs! A few morsels of prisoners' bread were on the floor and the mouse ran over to them, watching me carefully. I did not move and tried to convey to it, "But my friend, there's nothing to fear from me. We are both prisoners here."

During the next few weeks I discovered a whole new world. My companion had a family, and one day she brought in even smaller mice. If I kept very still, they would play in front of me. They came to know me well. They would eat the crumbs of bread I gave them, almost out of my hand.

In spite of this companionship, I fell into a coma, a state of semi-consciousness which lasted for about ten days. During this period I was not taken for interrogation, and I recollect being given injections by the prison doctor. I must have sat without moving for nearly a week in one of the damp cell corners, where I had feverish dreams and hallucinations. I saw, or thought I saw, shadows; moving silhouettes on the wall taking on human forms. I saw the head of Christ; then the head and shoulders of a Franciscan monk who held a Cross out towards me. I saw what seemed to be an angel, fluttering down in the clouds towards me, its long robes flowing out behind.

If these visions bewildered me, they also gave me hope of salvation.

On 23rd April, 1948, eight months after my arrival in Baden, by whence I had by then completely lost count of time, I was tried by a Russian court martial. Taken upstairs to a large room, I was forced to confront three Russian officers who sat behind a red cloth-covered table. I was charged with high treason and espionage against Hungary and the Soviet Union.

Between the pages of the extensive interrogation minutes slips of paper had been placed as markers, and as he turned the pages the court President put a series of sharp questions. He did not read the entire minutes; that would have taken weeks. Instead, he asked if I understood the selected paragraphs. I was amazed at the lies and falsifications. Sometimes I recognised a name, but most of the statements had never been uttered by me. I asked how all this nonsense had got into the minutes. With an ironical smile he said "This is your confession. In your own words."

It was now my turn to smile. "You appear to be taking these statements for granted" I said. "You are evidently already convinced of my guilt. There seems little point in my attempting to defend myself."

I had heard about the infamous "telegram tribunals" in which the prisoner is sentenced by telegram from Moscow, the *troika* method; I suspected that this was what had happened. I was sure that the telegram sentencing me lay there on the table beside the minutes. All these formalities and minute readings were a farce. I said that I had no means of calling witnesses; there was no counsel for my defence, although, according to Russian law, this was obligatory. "So, gentlemen," I said, "I am completely in your hands. You can do what you like with me. There seems little point in attempting to present my case. You evidently know my sentence already. You are my prosecutors, not my judges."

The President replied that I knew how to argue. "That is as it should be," he said. "You are a lawyer. But that makes your crime worse. As an educated man you should have used your knowledge in support of democracy."

The procedure of reading from the selected minutes lasted about an hour. To my amazement I then heard what seemed like words of comfort. "Do not be afraid," he said. "If you work well after your sentence in the punishment camp, and show a respectful attitude, it may be possible to grant clemency later. You may be freed within the borders of the Soviet Union. There you will be able to work as an equal with everyone else. You will be able to join in the noble work of building socialism. You will see what a more humane life you will have in the new society. After a while, you will realise that you are disillusioned with the capitalist world.

I was given twenty-five years' forced labour. In any other year I would have received the death penalty.

Neunkirchen, my first destination on the long journey to Russia, is on the Austro-Hungarian border; and here I was taken the next day, with a number of other convicted prisoners. Baden is not far from the British and American zones and many prisoners must have contemplated escape, so our hands were bound. I could hardly stand, I was so dizzy when I again saw the light of day.

After eight months in a dark cell, it is hard to describe how strange one feels when one comes out into the open. My first impression was of the colour, of its vividness and variety, the startling greenness of the fields, the rich blueness of the sky and the dazzling white of the whitewashed cottages. These colours struck me as if my retina had taken on another sensitivity, like that of a deep-water fish, attuned to the subtlest gradations of grey and black. I even felt, while waiting half an hour for the prison van, a strange longing to be back in my grey world with the mice and spiders, to return to the womb of the cell.

The transit centre in Neunkirchen had once been a Nazi "model prison". Hitler had operated there three years previously; now Stalin had taken over. It was surrounded by high brick walls capped with barbed wire, and in each corner of the courtyard were wooden towers where armed guards looked down on us. Here in this modern building, no expense had been spared. There were even fine beds of geraniums in the centre.

Here, for the first time since my arrest nearly twelve months previously, I again found human company. Other prisoners had undergone similar confinement, and our first words, as the key was turned in our new cell, were happy ones. The first phase of our torment was over, and we discussed, almost with clinical curiosity, our unpredictable future. Most of my new companions had by now acquired a kind of happy-go-lucky lightheartedness, almost an indifference to the free outside world.

All convicted prisoners were sent to Neunkirchen before being transported on to Russia. We were an assortment of nationalities. Our cell was soon filled until we numbered thirty-five, all caught up in the vast net which the Russians had cast into Central and Eastern Europe: Czechs, Slovaks, British, Rumanians, Hungarians, Americans, Austrians, Yugoslavs, Germans and even Russians, jostled one another and slept cheek by jowl. Each had his story to tell. Each described his capture and spoke indignantly of his alleged crime. Every day for weeks, groups of these assorted peoples would be gathered into what was known as an étape, or transportation assembly, and sent off in cattle or prisoner trucks for their distant goal, the Russian work camps.

Among this hotch-potch of nations I soon heard of tragedies other than my own, and I became accustomed to sympathising with other prisoners over their fate. A new critical sense or awareness possessed me, and I realised that I could never have learned so much about human life in the freedom of the world outside. Here, in this inferno of suffering, I heard of ordeals beside which my own paled into insignificance. I even gained a peace of mind. I was aware that a great new human migration was taking place around me, and that in this ferment, this twentieth century avalanche, I was only a minute speck.

Chapter 3

PRISONS ON WHEELS - December 1948

Each of the étapes or stopping places that I have previously described contained prisoners, guilty, broadly speaking, of one particular "crime". I and a number of others were in the worst category, as "British and American spies," and it took some months before there were enough of us to be worth moving. We had to wait from May until December, when our cells had become so crowded that we were sleeping on top of one another.

One wintry morning we were ordered to change into old Russian uniforms. The hands and feet of the "most dangerous" (including myself) were bound with wire, and we were thrown into waiting lorries like sacks of potatoes. Some six hundred of us were then conveyed by convoy to Neunkirchen railway station. There, a special prisoners' train was waiting. It consisted of about fifty wagons, each equipped with thirty-five bunks, and staffed with three guards. These guards lived on the trains, accompanying prisoners back and forth across Russia. Having lost all human feeling; one could read the callousness and brutality on their faces. They warned us that any attempt at escape would result in instant death, and when we reached the Hungarian border, one of them said "We're now travelling through Hungary. You're Hungarian, so don't give any trouble or shout to your people. It'll be a quick death, if you do." I had hoped that the wire would be taken off my hands and feet, but it was removed only from my legs. Fortunately, another prisoner, a friendly Austrian eased my wrists a little as we crossed Hungary. To prevent contact with the local population, even the guards were confined in their compartments. On reaching Budapest they took even greater precautions. We were made to lie motionless on our bunks for hours, until the train left. On the way, I heard the Hungarian voices of the railwaymen tapping the wheels beneath our wagon. I was unable to tell them that I was bound for slavery in Russia.

Conditions were appalling. There was no water and we used a hole at the end of the wagon as a toilet. During the long winter journey across central Europe older prisoners often missed the hole, and the wagon was soon awash with filth. It was embarrassing that some of the bunks contained women and even more so that those of us whose hands were tied had to be assisted as we relieved ourselves. But we were so exhausted, that we soon became indifferent.

Produced in a kitchen wagon at the end of the train, our food consisted of watery cabbage soup containing two or three leaves, maize soup or occasionally, cold fish. Some of the older prisoners were soon in agony through eating the salt fish without anything to drink. Those whose hands were tied had to be fed by others.

Even though it was mid winter, the wagons had no form of heating, and we were wearing old, threadbare Russian uniforms. Some Russian prisoners evolved an ingenious way of making a fire. They undid the seams of their caps and jackets and extracted small bits of cotton wool and fluff which had collected there. This they twisted into compact masses. They then removed their boots, and ground the cottonwool so violently on the floor beneath their soles that it produced friction and caught alight. Some found twigs or small pieces of wood with which for a short time they could warm their hands.

During the four day journey, five prisoners died including a young Ukrainian with whom I had made friends in Neunkirchen. He had been dead a day when we reached the Russian frontier, but the guards left his corpse in the wagon with the other prisoners. "Its a cold winter,"one of them said. "He won't stink for a day or two."

At the border with Russia the railway gauge changed, and we were transferred to Russian cattle wagons with windows sealed by iron plates. We also had new guards who checked everything again. They were particularly interested in our personal belongings, and I realised that toothbrushes, cigarette holders and socks were luxuries in Russia. They stole these, and we heard them arguing as to who should get what.

The journey to Lvov, took two days. The city is only two hundred and seventy kilometers inside Russia. The area was still full of Ukrainian partisans, and large-scale skirmishes were continually taking place in the mountains and valleys. The authorities were careful not to allow prisoners' trains to run at night through the mountain passes and lonely forests of the Carpathians, where they could easily be attacked. Some prisoners said that supplies of food and ammunition were regularly parachuted from the West.

Our Ukrainian fellow-prisoners told us that orders were sent from partisan headquarters to smaller groups. They explained how reports and news were distributed; how Russian trains were derailed, depots and Collective farms attacked; how the local inhabitants were compelled to give the partisans food, lodging and information. Had they not done this, they said, they would have been attacked as traitors. Some of the Ukrainian prisoners in our wagon had been sentenced by the Russians for giving shelter, if only for a few hours, to a partisan, or for having offered food. For such a crime, a fifteen or twenty year sentence was not uncommon.

The Ukrainian partisans often attacked prison trains at night and liberated their inmates. This was why our train stood the whole of each night in stations together with other engines, all blowing their whistles, as if, by so doing, they might help each other's morale.

Russian wagons had stoves, but the few logs which were thrown in at night, burned within about an hour. As we crossed the Carpathians the cold became more intense. On arrival at Lvov, those prisoners who had caught pneumonia, and were still alive, were bundled together in separate trucks and taken to the prison hospital.

We all had great hopes of Lvov. Skilful propaganda by the Russian political officers in Neunkirchen may have been responsible for this, for the news had spread that the inhuman prison conditions we had lived under during the interrogations would cease when we reached the Soviet Union. Most of us believed that a comparatively better future, even if it meant hard work, awaited us. The Russian prisoners also spoke of better conditions, saying that we sould be taken to the industrial centres of the Ukraine.

But our treatment in the Lvov transit camp was, if anything, worse than it had been in Austria. When we arrived at the station, yelling secret police officials bundled us into large black vans, twenty-five or thirty squeezed into space for twelve. Arms and legs hung out at the back, but the guards simply slammed the doors on them.

At the bottom of the pile of prisoners, I was hardly able to breathe.

The most significantly memorable feature of the Lvov transit camp was my introduction to the "bandits", a ruthless organisation which flourished both inside and outside the prisons of Russia. Not unlike the Klu Klux Klan, it terrorised prisoners throughout the Soviet Union. In ways, these men were more powerful than the guards.

Our Ukrainian friends had already spoken of the murders and robberies the bandits had committed in the camps, and after only a week in Lvov, I realised that they were among us. I learned to recognise them by the way they congregated and attacked fellow prisoners, generally for their food or clothes. When any of us protested, they warned us to keep quiet; if we did not, they would kill us.

"Just you fit in", one of them said to me "or you'll be in for trouble. You Europeans have had a better time than we've ever had. We've never had anything. Leave us to get what we want the way we want!"

It took months to understand the psychology of these sinister men, perhaps a hundred thousand of them spread out over the entire penal network of Russia, who were a law unto themselves; and to realise that the prison authorities were unable to control them. Had I then read Dostoievsky's stories from *The House of the Dead*, I would have known that these bandits are indigenous to Russia; they had existed in Tsarist times.

One morning, an old Ukrainian peasant complained that a food parcel he had received from his relations had been stolen during the night. We knew what had happened, because some of the bandits had been eyeing his food the previous night. They had withdrawn to a corner of the cell, as was their habit, and talked quietly among themselves.

A courageous young Ukrainian who saw that the old man could not defend himslef, accused the bandits of theft. "We've had enough of you brutes", he said. "We won't have any more stealing in this cell. You're a minority among us. You've been doing what you like until now. Now you're going to give him back his parcel."

We were so encouraged by this that when the bandits attacked him, we came to his rescue. We tore the planks from the bunks, and lashed out at the bandits, who retaliated. Blood soon flowed. A blow on my head from another young Ukrainian which almost knocked me out. (He later told me I was so filthy and unrecognisable that he had mistaken me for a bandit!) Some of the Ukrainians threw heavy earthenware mugs at the bandits, one of whom received

a broken mug in the face. Another collapsed with a huge gash in his neck. After fifteen minutes of pandemonium, the door burst open and in strode guards armed with steel bars. Immediately they began lashing about in all directions. I received another blow which I felt for weeks afterwards. At the end of the skirmish, two prisoners were carried off unconscious, a Ukrainian had his ear torn off, and another man's nose and arm were broken.

During an inquiry the following day, we were each examined by the authorities. Our Ukrainian comrades warned us not to incriminate the bandits, because we could never be sure when we might again meet them. The bandits' bush telegraph between the various camps was very effective, as I was later to discover. "People have been murdered," the Ukrainian told us, "when they arrive in a new prison, for denouncing a bandit in another prison thousands of miles away."

We consequently told the prison authorities that a quarrel had broken out, in the heat of which two factions had formed, both equally to blame. The interrogating officer knew only too well what had happened, but he just smiled, and no one was punished. Such then, was my introduction to Russian prisons. In most gaols, the prisoner's worst enemy is the gaoler. Here we found a more insidious enemy among our fellow captives.

In the new year, before the journey to Central Russia, I was medically examined. The doctors were security policewomen wearing MVD officers' uniforms, one of whom became interested in my personal possessions. Our Russian gaolers were often prepared to give us food in exchange for some personal belonging from the West; and this female coveted the wool blanket my sister had sent me on my arrest. She told one of my cell mates that if he could persuade me to hand it over, she would prescribe extra food rations for him. This man, Zoltan Varga, was in a very poor state of health. I knew that he needed more to eat before the long journey to Central Russia, so I gave it to him. For this he acquired half a pound of margarine, a spoonful of millet, and about two ounces of bread a day. I soon learned that there was really little point in keeping such possessions, because sooner or later they would be stolen by the bandits.

The day before we left for Central Russia, I saw some girls, probably all under fourteen, exercising in the prison yard. I was informed that they had been sentenced for distributing "Ukrainian nationalist propaganda". That children should be treated as criminals, in the same prison as the bandits, seemed to me the depths of barbarity. I saw a prisoner hanging from a barbed wire fence with his stomach ripped wide open by the wire. These young girls had to pass beside him on their way to exercise.

It was not until March 1949 that special officials came to select us according to our physique and capacity to work. We were made to stand in front of them naked, and the prison doctors informed them about each of us. One prisoner they considered fit for the Arctic or the forests of the Far East; another, better suited for the Volga district; another, for the marshes where new canals were being built; the coal mines of Vorkuta in the tundra, or perhaps Central Asian metal mines. When my turn came, I was assigned to Labour Camp 10. I had no concept of the significance of this or where the place was.

We left Lvov one morning early in March, 1949, in the depths of a Russian winter. In spite of this, some of us still thought of escaping. Little did we comprehend what the word 'escape' meant in those endless plains in winter.

The prison wagons were larger than those used in Western Europe. They had been sent from camps in Central Russia to collect us, and were specially equipped for prisoners. They were much wider than previous ones, with three separate tiers of bunks, two along the sides and one in the centre of each compartment. There was an iron stove, and a primitive lavatory at the end of the carriage. The train was also equipped with a kitchen wagon, but during the first days we got no hot food, only salted fish and less than a kilo of black bread. There was no water. It may seem strange that anyone surrounded by such expanses of snow should feel the torments of thirst; but we enthusiastically scratched down the hoar frost from the inside walls of the wagon, and sucked it.

There were some eighty prisoners in our carriage,

and there was an immediate struggle for bunks. Everyone wanted the warmer top tiers. Older prisoners and Europeans like ourselves were less skilled at such struggles and soon found ourselves left with the lower ones.

The methods used to guard the train were very elaborate. Between the wagons special platforms for guards and machine-gun emplacements had been constructed, above which powerful searchlights were placed. There were guards in each wagon, some of whom had dogs. Telephones linked them with their commander's vehicle. Our Ukrainian comrades proundly confided to us that these precautions were necessary while we were in the Ukraine, among their partisans.

The first night we were sure that these partisans had attacked. Brakes were applied and the train stopped convulsively. We heard feverish shouts, dogs barking and orders yelled hoarsely from one end of the train to the other. The door of our wagon was thrown open. Security guards rushed in and ordered us to leave our bunks and assemble in one corner. Prisoners slow to obey received a sharp blow from the large wooden hammers they brandished. The guards then meticulously examined the bunks and floorboards. We hoped that the partisans had raided. But it was only a test. They checked if we had made holes in the walls, or had tried to loosen the boards.

Like some armoured convoy, our slave train progressed through the famous forests of Briansk. Everywhere, on all sides, was forest, stretching from Galicia and the Carpathians to Moscow, over two thousand kilometres ahead. It was only now that I understood the meaning of distance in Russia, and a new despondency, a feeling of utter hopelessness overcame me.

At first we passed towns and villages baring a

certain resemblance to those in Europe. But they soon degenerated into groups of small delapidated dwellings whose inhabitants, in rags and tatters, indicated that conditions were worse here than in Poland or the Ukraine. My native countryside, with its wooded hills and valleys and fertile plains, the Puszta, was like Canaan to this.

The older prisoners suffered most during the twelve-day journey. They could not control themselves in the intense cold, and the smell in the wagon soon became unbearable. I especially recall a Ukrainian who had been sentenced for helping the partisans. He told me that he had unwisely returned from America in the thirties having emigrated there and having amassed a small fortune, and had bought a farm in Galicia. He had survived the German occupation and when the Ukrainian partisans asked for food and shelter he gladly gave it. "Anyway, he said, "if I had not given it, they would have taken it. I am an old man, my wife is dead, and my daughters were not in the house. I was alone. What could I do? I'm over seventy-four. What have I to expect now from life? I am ready to die. May the Good Lord take me!"

Two days later I found him lying beside me in the early morning, motionless, his eyes wide open, staring; his body was stiff, and he had evidently been dead for some hours.

We had to travel on with his body for several days. When we arrived at our destination, I learned that there were several other corpses on the train.

By now I was beginning to lose control of my own body too, passing water in my sleep and waking to find my trousers frozen to the floor. At first, I tried to conceal the problem. When I realised it was happening to everyone else, however, I discussed it even though there was little we could do to help each other.

On the seventh day we reached Moscow. We spent forty-eight hours while the wagon was shunted about in various goods yards on the edge of the city. Self opinionated officials examined us. They went from wagon to wagon, smiling sardonically as they counted us like sheep.

After Moscow, the scene changed; the endless forests gave way to equally endless and featureless plains, across which we continued to travel for three days. During the last two we were given no food, and the Ukrainians said that the guards were selling our miserable rations to civilians at the stations through which we passed. So bad was local food that the population would gladly pay for our dry salted fish, ground oats and maize. Even our frozen military bread found customers.

Towards the end of the third day, the railway line petered out in a land of low bushes and marshes. Someone cried from a bunk above, "The camps are ahead! The camps are ahead!"

Anxious to see these notorious camps where we might have to spend the rest of our lives we all became immensely excited.

Chapter 4

QUARANTINE - March 1949

We looked out through the grilles, and saw a maze of wooden palisades, hutments, watch-towers, miles of barbed wire, and groups of prisoners in torn, quilted clothes accompanied by guards with dogs. As the train slowly moved on, we passed at least ten of these camps. We were in a new environment, a kind of national park, a human zoo.

The perimeter of Camp 10 consisted of a seven metre high palisade which was surrounded by barbed wire projecting inwards and outwards. Outside this there was a second barbed wire fence in which were a number of watch-towers, each about a hundred metres apart. On these hung two metre iron rods, which the guards would clang from time to time to inform the neighbouring towers that they were alert. The corner turrets were equipped with machine-guns and searchlights.

At these gates, I saw for the first time another curious feature of camp life with which I was to become familiar; this was a piece of birch wood shaped like a slate. The guards used it when counting at roll calls. They scratched the numbers on it, which they would later erase with a piece of broken glass. This indicated a shortage of paper in the Soviet Union. The only writing materials available in the camp were such bits of birch and sharp instruments such as pieces of flint or glass which served as pencils.

On our arrival the camp inmates, mainly old and crippled prisoners, were loitering about staring at us;

they were sharply ordered back to their huts. Some of our companions had become so weak during the journey that they had to be carried on stretchers by their friends. We were taken to a large barracks which had been divided from the rest of the camp by a barbed wire fence. This was the quarantine barracks for new prisoners.

As we waited, some of my companions went up to the barbed wire fence, but the guards in the watch-towers waved them away. One prisoner was not quick enough, so the guards shot in the air behind him. I was to discover that in this camp they were very quick on the trigger; if they disliked a prisoner they would shoot round or near him. When the administrative arrangements such as the checking of names, numbers and ages had been completed, we were divided into groups and taken to the baths.

The temperature was thirty degrees below zero centigrade, and even in the bathroom it was below freezing point. We had to strip completely and were then admitted to the bath, a large wooden tub three metres high and four metres in diameter, where we were given two pails of water and a small bar of brown soap. Meanwhile, our clothes were taken away by elderly prisoners who had to search the pockets and disinfect them.

It was so cold that we all washed rapidly, only to find that we had to wait naked and shivering for half an hour until our clothes were returned. As we dressed, one of the elderly prisoners who had been in charge of the clothes, seemed anxious to talk to me. He spoke German, and said how sorry he was to see a young man like me in such a place. "Do you know what kind of camp this is?" he asked.

I said I imagined it was like any other Russian concentration camp. I supposed they were all much the same.

"No", he said. "You are in the camp for the worst political offenders. Old Tsarist officers like myself, dangerous spies, high Communist officials who have fallen into disgrace, Leninists, Trotskyists, scientists who have offended authority. That is why this camp is nearer Moscow than the others. Not in Siberia. They want to keep an eye on you." He looked at me intently, and then said, "No one has ever left this camp alive."

He told me that he was an ex-staff officer who had fought the Reds during the revolution. He was captured and imprisoned, but released in the twenties. Later, in Stalin's time, he was imprisoned again, and sent here. All his relatives were dead, so he had no desire to leave. He doubted if he could ever find a place again in the modern world. No one would now understand him; he was only waiting for God to relieve him of his suffering.

"All the same," he said, "I can't bear to see young chaps like you in this camp. You still have something to live for. We are all suffering for a better, Christian way of life. All we can do is to accept the suffering God imposes. You, my boy must regard your fate as a good Christian should. Suffer it with dignity and patience." He was so moved by his own words that he started to cry.

I told him that it was not enough to passively accept suffering; I agreed that we must keep our faith in God, and said that I knew He would not allow such injustice to go on indefinitely. "I know," I said, "that we shall live to see better days. In a free and happier world. We shall enjoy life again."

This conversation left a deep impression on me. Although it depressed me, to meet such a man was a help in the first hours of my life in these camps. His religious faith strengthened the conviction developed since my arrest, that the only way I could bear suffering would be by putting myself into the hands of God.

New prisoners had to undergo quarantine, partly to submit to medical inspection which would indicate what work we were to be allocated and partly, I believe, to prevent communication with other prisoners, and spreading optimistic stories about the West. This was psychologically ingenious for after a month or six weeks, any newly introduced information was out of date and our enthusiasm and desire to spread such news had diminished.

As we idly underwent our period of quarantine, and as we ran out of personal stories to share with each other, a mood of general depression replaced our mutual optimism. Some of us were more cold than hungry; others more hungry than cold. The food was obnoxious - thin cabbage soup, mush from half hulled grain, and half a kilo of bread, a heavy black dough which contained fifty per cent water. Our ration was particularly small because this was an invalid camp, for the weaker prisoners in the light working categories. As a result there was continuous bartering. Those who had managed to bring a scarf, a vest, or piece of warm clothing, would exchange it for a few pieces of dry bread. I exchanged some of my clothes in this way but I regretted it. For a few hours' relief from hunger I lost a warm pullover.

There was no heating in the camp, but one advantage of there being overcrowding was that, as we slept almost on top of each other, we generated our own warmth. Bloodstains from previous conflicts with bed-bugs were visible over all the bunks, and we were soon also fighting the losing battle against them.

We used snow for bath water. For tooth brushes we used our fingers, and soap for paste.

A guard had been placed at the entrance of the quarantine block to prevent us talking with other prisoners. Because prisoners in the past had often attacked guards and stolen their weapons, he was not armed. Sometimes, however, if he was not looking, we would approach the wire fince in the quarantine barracks, and exchange a few words with the old men who were clearing away the snow. This was often so high around the palisades that it even reached the top of the fence. It made escape easier in the winter, and explained why the older men, incapable of getting away, were regularly sent out to clear it as it fell. Some were Turkmen or Kazaksanian and I had great difficulty in distinguishing between the various eastern faces I saw across the palisades.

After two weeks, the snow fell so heavily that even the quarantine prisoners themselves were used to clear it near the railway lines. We were still wearing our tattered old Russian uniforms which were poor protection against this climate; I had an overcoat which was tied together with bits of string. Our clothes were often fastened in this way because, when we were frequently searched the action was conducted in such a brusque manner that the buttons were ripped off. Later, we were given caps padded with cotton wool, and old military boots.

As the days of quarantine passed, some of the more daring prisoners who had spent years in the camp sneaked into our barracks to talk and to find out about us. One of these was a Hungarian cobbler, a Communist, who had fled to Russia in a fit of idealism. I liked him, but my friends warned me that he might be an informer sent in to find out what we conversed about.

My greatest surprise and delight was to meet Miklos Csomos, who had worked in the same underground movement during the war. I have mentioned that, during my interrogation in Baden, the Russians had threatened me with the "same fate as Csomos's." But when we met, we didn't at first recognise each other. He had once been a huge bear-like fellow, and I remembered him radiating good health and energy. This man had hollow cheeks; the great frame seemed shurnken and emaciated. This ghost of the man I had previously known approached me. Only his irrepressible good humour and love of life remained. On recognition, he roared with laughter and slapped me on the back.

"Raphael!" he cried. "You look as if you had gone through a mangle. What have they done to you?"

What have they done to you?" I asked. "You must have lost five stone."

"Yes," he said philosophically. The food here is not exactly nourishing. Not like those meals we used to eat together on the Margaret Island. But it's marvellous to see you again, you old rogue! What did they get you for?"

I related my story to him, and talked about our work for the western allies and the political views he had shared with my father and me. "Yes, yes," he said. "The mad son of a mad father! We all stood up to the Germans. Now we are standing up to the Russians. And here we are! This is what Liberal politics have done to us!"

Miklos had been sentenced to death in Hungary by the Communists, and had been kept in the death cell for forty days. During this period he never knew if, when the cell door opened, he was to be taken into the yard and, like many whose cries he had heard, executed. His sentence had finally been commuted and here he was; serving a term of twenty-five years' hard labour.

He had arrived some years before me, and the camp administration had soon discovered his qualifications as a dentist. They now used him as their family doctor. Working in the hospital block, he held a privileged position which enabled him to obtain drugs from the special police stock, and permits for the sick exempting them from work. In the days to come, Miklos did everything he could to help us. When the end of our quarantine was approaching, a Russian general named Sergienko visited our barracks and made a short speech, asking if we had any complaints. Two Lithuanian boys came forward, claiming that they should not be given the same punishment as the adults and asked to be transferred to a youth camp. They said they had been too young to know what they were doing, and courageously expressed their dislike of Communism. The older prisoners who understood what was going on (the Lithuanians spoke Russian, because Lithuania had been under Soviet rule for some years, and they had learnt Russian at school) held their breath, fearing that the Russian general would lose his temper and that punishments would follow for everybody. But the general showed no emotion.

"You are old enought to know you committed a crime," he said. "You are, in fact, doubly guilty, because you received a good education in Lithuania. This should have taught you that it is a crime to engage in partisan activities against the Soviet Union. Being properly educated, you are regarded as adults. That is why you have been punished as adults."

He then went on to warn us that we were all here to be punished, and that work was about to begin. He assured us that the administration knew how to run the camp, and that they had means of finding out our most secret thoughts and plans.

Chapter 5

THE PRISON WORLD - April 1949

The Dubrov area formed only one of the Soviet Union's many concentration camp centres. These centres were spread across the whole country, as far north as the Kolyma Camps of North-Eastern Siberia, where gold was mined in the tundra. There was the Vorkuta region, also in the north, concentrating largely on the mining of anthracite; the Petchora region, in the north-east, with ordinary coal mines; the virgin forest area near Taiga above Lake Baikal, producing timber and asbestos, and the Altai Mountains near Kazakhstan where quicksilver, copper and lead were found. To the south was the Karaganda concentration camp area. There were further groupings in Turkmenia and in the northern Caucasus.

These other areas had relatively healthy climates, whereas Dubrov area was in marshland invaded by mosquitoes in summer, and damp and cold in winter. It has been chosen, as the ex-Tsarist officer had said for "political" prisoners, many of whom were older men, incapable of the hard manual labour needed for mining. Work here was largely maintenance of bridges and roads, snow clearing, of the unloading or railway wagons. The wagons arrived from the surrounding forests with timber for the other work camps in the Dubrov area, some of which had woodwork shops and furniture factories. While in quarantine, the work capacity of each of us was assessed by the *nariarchiks*, or inner camp administrators, who then allotted us our places in labour brigades.

These *nariarchiks* were the confidence men of the regime and were selectd from among the prisoners. They were usually Russians, or men from the Soviet Union's other territories, who had been sentenced for minor offences. They were exempted from outside work, and carried out administrative duties within the camp. They supplied the authorities with regular reports about the morale of the prisoners and with other confidential information. They were also responsible for staffing the labour brigades, to whom they forwarded orders received from the central officer. They were all loyal to the administration, and were prepared to undertake any task, hoping for an amnesty or at least for an improvement in their position, in reward for faithful service. This was naive, because they should have learnt by now how the Soviet system worked, how little it cared about anyone who had lost its favour. But they obstinately clung to their expectations.

One morning, a *nariarchik* visited our block with his adjutants, and allotted us to various brigades, according to our fitness. The secret police made a final search of our barracks and then, after a month of quarantine, we graduated into the working and social world of Soviet Concentration Camp 10.

We reported to our brigadier who had received a list of names, and he consigned us to our tasks. Both the *nariarchik* and they were prisoners in semi-official position, the former administrative, the latter executive. Some of these brigadiers were extremely unpleasant; but ours, who was half Finnish, was helpful and even well disposed towards us Hungarians. He pointed out that our two nations, the Finns and Hungarians, were connected and that he was glad I was working under him.

The day's work started with reveille at five, when it was still dark. Breakfast began half an hour later and continued till seven; the first to eat were the brigades going out to work. The invalids employed on duties inside the camp went to the canteen after the muster roll, or *proverka*, had been taken at seven.

This muster was strictly observed, and all had to be present. Even the cripples, of which there were many in Camp 10, had to line up in the snow like everybody else, while their numbers were recorded. Reports containing the exact figures were then telephoned to central administration.

Breakfast and other meals were served in a wooden barrack hall to which kitchen and pantries were attached. We sat on benches at long tables, and the brigadier's appointed men brought us tin bowls of food. The system by which inmates queued for food at the kitchen window had been tried, but had not worked; some prisoners went twice whereas others got nothing. Breakfast consisted of a thin mush of half-hulled grain and the daily bread ration of six hundred grammes. Some of us were so hungry that we ate the whole day's portion at the beginning of the day.

After breadkfast, the brigade leaders received their instructions for the day's work. We were ordered to the camp perimeter where an inner gate was opened, and we were admitted into the "letting out" boxes. When the gates closed behind us, those of the outer fences were opened, and we made our way through. Outside the palisade, groups of armed guards with dogs awaited us and after being counted again - we had to step forward in rows of five - we marched off to work. We toiled till half past twelve, and then had an hour's break. If were were near the camp, we returned for lunch; otherwise our mid-day meal was brought to us by the older, invalid prisoners. The afternoon shift lasted from two to six. In theory we had a twelve-hour working day; in practice, it was several hours longer, either because special work had to be finished on time, or because we were delayed by the interminable roll calls and searchings.

Supper consisted of the same kind of mushy soup we had had for breakfast, togther with four or five komsa, small salt fish two inches long which were sometimes called "Russian oysters"; these added nourishment. They were served between six and eight and usually to the old people first before the working brigades returned.

One of our number, a doctor, calculated the calorific value of our rations. The invalids, he said, received 1200 calories daily, including bread and sugar; the workers, just under 1500. On paper it looked much better. The workers were supposed, officially, to receive 2800 calories; but by the time it reached them it was always below 1500. Corruption was so universal that food was stolen at every stage of its delivery. The MVD, as well as camp administration, were guilty of this. The kitchen chef, the stockkeeper and the **nariarchiks**, also came in for their share.. There was no point in complaining, because prisoners were not trusted, nor were we expected to tell the truth. The calories we received were half our minimum requirement.

Under-nourishment was responsible for tuberculosis among the younger prisoners, as well as distrophea, a kind of slow starvation which caused a gradual weakening of the body. They collapsed at work, and had to be taken to hospital where they were permitted a few days on better food. Two or three weeks later they would be back at work. There was quite some traffic of people with distrophea continually going in and out of hospital. We often observed the skeleton-like figures of tubercular patients wandering about in the hospital enclosure, where they were allowed a little exercise. In summer, when their bodies were uncovered, their thighs looked as thin as normal shins. In the bath, I was once horrified to see my neighbour's protuding bones, only to realise that he was observing exactly the same phenomenon in me.

In the evenings, if we were not too exhausted, we would attempt to organise cultural groups to occupy our minds. The most popular activity was the learning of foreign languages, especially English. This was, of course, strictly forbidden. English was the language of Russia's greatest enemies and, the authorities argued, anyone caught learning it must desire victory for capitalism. Even Russian could not be studied, as it might help prisoners in their attempts to escape. Any prisoner found trying to write the language was punished with ten or fifteen days **karker,** time spent in a cold, damp, semi-dark underground punishment cell.

In spite of such a threat, many prisoners were prepared to take the risk in order to pick up a few words of English. Many also studied French and German. I taught Hungarian to Estonians and Lithuanians, both of whom had a great talent for languages.

Some of the guards also wanted to learn foreign languages; where it could be done secretly, we taught them. Miklos Csomos, my dentist friend, didn't know much English, but pretended to the guards that he was an expert, and was giving three of them lessons when our group arrived. Now and again he invented completely spurious words, which he himself also had to memorise.

A Japanese metallurgical engineer, Okano also became a regular visitor to our barrack block because of his desire to learn English. He had been sentenced to twenty-five years' imprisonment for espionage. When the Russians arrived in Korea in 1945, they found that he knew too much about Korean politics to be left; so they charged him with spying for the Americans. He was a shy man, but he became a part of our Baltic circle, and I believe he enjoyed it; if such a word can be used in a Russian concentration camp. We often used to sit together smoking a little squat pipe made from bread, which I had dried in an oven, handing it from one to the other and talking English. He told me about his metallurgical inventions, most of which were still experimental. He had most novel ideas about artificial manure, and problems with other chemical.

Another friend was Harry Anderson, a Lithuanian, who had lost a leg while fighting for the Germans during the war.

After the conflict he visited a family in the American Zone of West Germany, to inform them of the death of their son who had died beside him in battle. They grew so fond of him that they adopted him in place of their own, and he married their daughter. All went well until the American secret service, who employed him because of his knowledge of Russian, started sending him over to the Russian zone. The fact that his leg was missing helped him on these incursions as people were sorry for him. But he was caught, and handed over to the Russians.

At nine o'clock as each day came to an end, *odboy* (Retreat), was sounded and everyone had to be by their beds. There was a staff inspection or roll and prisoners who were absent were subject to *karker*.

One night we heard shots outside the camp, followed by snarling and growling. My more experienced fellow prisoners knew what was happening. Wolves, driven towards the camps by hunger, had attacked the watchdogs and torn them to pieces. We were delighted because we hated the camp dogs. Trained to hunt men, they were always loose at night along the palisades. There they trotted back and forth along wires to which their chains were attached, giving them considerable freedom of movement. If there was an attempted escape, they would alarm the guards.

When our quarantine was over, the bunks in the block to which I was assigned were so crowded that we were unable to sleep on our backs. We had to rest on our sides, packed like so many sardines, all facing the same way so as not to breathe into our neighbour's face. If in the middle of the night we felt uncomfortable, we somehow turned round and woke the next person; he, in turn, woke his neighbour and so on until everyone was facing the other way. This called for a good deal of tolerance, and each group of sleeping prisoners had to be good friends.

A lot depended, too, on the fact that some bodies were somewhat more odourous than others. After having a number of dirty and very smelly sleeping companions, I located Anonos Bruzhas, a Lithuanian who was most agreeable and had a good sense of humour. As a boy, he had almost been executed during the Russian Revolution, simply because he used to turn the pages for the organist in the local church.

It is often said that the only way to know someone really well is to sleep with them. However, the usual presumptions did not apply here, although I shall be mentioning homosexuality later on in the book. By sleeping next to Bruzhas, I got to know him very well.

Before the war, Bruzhas had become a well-known figure, as the owner and editor of the biggest Lithuanian newspaper. Liberal, and concerned chiefly with agriculture, his was the most popular newspaper among the smallholders and middle classes.

He used to laugh about this and say, "I wish I'd stuck to my organ playing. It doesn't get you into trouble like running a newspaper does. After we leave this place, I advise you, Raphael, to take a job in Hungary as a village organist. You'll be happy for the rest of your life."

As well as a sense of humour, Bruzhas was curiously fastidious and had a particular desire for order and cleanliness. He told me that this had, on one occasion in 1918, saved his life. He had been taken for interrogation by the Communist Security Police who were then on the look-out for people with a "bourgeois background." The police station had had two exits, one of which was filthy and the other, relatively clean. The official finally got tired of questioning him and ordered, pointing to the dirty door, "All right, get out there!"

Bruzhas had laughed and said facetiously, "No, it's filthy. I'd prefer to go through the other door. It looks cleaner."

The official irritably replied: "Go where you like, you bloody bourgeois!"

Bruzhas later discovered that the dirty door led to underground cells where prisoners were shot, whereas he had chosen the one into the street! "Things were like that in 1918", he said. "But they were very different when I was arrested this time, I can tell you."

Nevertheless, because Bruzha's family lived in Lithuania, he received the preferential treatment meted out to Russians, and he was allowed to receive parcels from home. During the previous year, he had even been permitted to exchange two letters with his family. The food parcels, which he generously shared with the rest of us, made a great difference. Even after years of Soviet occupation, the Lithuanian food parcels were still of good quality. The brigadiers generally expected a share of the contents, and because I was Bruzhas's friend I, too, was better treated.

The commencement of our work programme fortunately coincided with the spring, a season which in Russia lasts only a week or two before the continental summer sets in. The sudden changes of climate, from bitter cold to stifling heat, are most disagreeable when one is unaccustomed to them. But the sight of all the flowers in bloom that first spring was elating, and we were glad to be out in the forests and fields. Such was the hunger of some of the prisoners that they cut fresh grass, ground it with stones, sprinkled salt on it, and devoured it. They claimed it was full of vitamins. The other springtime delicacies were the buds of birch trees. When the guards were not looking, we descended on these like whe clouds of locusts, denuding the trees as far as our hands could reach. We also picked and ate berries growing in the forest, and took some back to our older friends and the sick prisoners in the camp.

There were other forms of nourishment which I found less attractive such as cockchafers and various kinds of forest beetle. I even saw old people catching flies and eating them. For liquid refreshment, we drank the sap of the birch, the national tree of Russia. This was forbidden, but many of the prisoners had become very skilful in extracting the liquid. They made small incisions in the tree-trunks and tied cans below to catch it as it seeped out. It was thicker than water, and had a sweetish, pleasant taste. Other prisoners often ate industrial vaseline which they spread on the black bread, and persuaded themselves that it tasted like bacon dripping.

Miklos Csomos, who used to accompany us on foraging expeditions, claimed, as a medical man, to know all the vitamins. When I expressed my horror at the old men eating flies, he said, "They're much wiser than you. Flies are full of proteins. Don't think about it as you eat them. Chew them well, and they'll do you a power of good."

Sometimes while we ate these strange foods, Miklos would regale us with tales of imaginary Barmecide feasts. He had been a great epicure in Budapest before the war, and spoke of caviare and *boeuf Stroganoff, Saltinbocca alla Romana*, Chateau-Yquem and Chambolle-Musigny in such terms as to make our mouths water. He would describe in great detail, the most superb banquets he intended to give himself when he returned home from Russia. This optimistic approach as to his future at least made us laugh. On one occasion we were able to satisfy even his gastronomic tastes. A covey of partridges, blinded by the sun, flew into our barbed wire one morning, leaving three dead against the palisade. These the camp baker prepared, cooked and shared with his friends. I have never relished partridges so much before or since.

The guards who accompanied our working parties were uncouth men, whose motto roughly translated "Shoot first and ask afterwards." There had been a number of unnecessary shootings, especially where there had been simmering feuds between individual guards and prisoners. As a consequence, the infamous *zapret* or forbidden-zone system was introduced for working parties. A *zapret* zone was defined by signposts, beyond which no prisoner might walk without permission. Equally, as long as a prisoner remained within the *zapret*, the guard was not allowed to fire at him - except, of course, where a prisoner deliberately attacked a guard (many prisoners, apart from the bandits, were so desperate that they sometimes did). Nor was the guard allowed to interfere with the speed or quality of a prisoner's work; these were the responsibilities of the brigadier. I mention these details because of a tragic incident which occurred not long after we started work.

One of my colleagues was a Ukrainian who was always taunting an unpopular guard. He was courageous, but also unwise, because the guard hated him, and was waiting to have his revenge. One afternoon the Ukrainian went into the *zapret* zone to relieve himself. He had presumably obtained permission, but as he was returning, we heard a burst of machine-gun fire followed by a scream. He lay on the ground, throwing himself from side to side, howling and bleeding. The guard had shot him inside the *zapret* zone. We started to run to his aid, but the guard shrieked that if we moved another step he would also shoot us. It was not long before the Ukrainian rolled over convulsively, and breathed his last.

Another guard went to fetch a truck and we were ordered back to work. Fortunately, most of the day's work was done, for none of us felt like doing any more after this. A cart was brought from a nearby collective farm, and the guards ordered us to lift the corpse on to it.

Returning to camp, we were frequently halted and the gaps between each marching column were checked and lengthened. Spades, which were the only "weapons" we had, were collected and carried separately by three prisoners. Such incidents led to bloody riots, and the guards took no chances. In fact, once, when the prisoners were marching home after such an incident, they had dragged the offending guard into their ranks, and finished him off with their hands. We had to wait a quarter of an hour that evening before being admitted to camp, where other armed guards had been called up, in case of trouble. Dogs were let loose within, and we were confined to barracks. Later, we were allowed to go to the toilets but only in supervised groups, following a special route. No gathering of prisoners was allowed, and no one could leave his barrack block without permission. This was the first incident of its kind I had witnessed in Camp 10.

Later I was also to experience as unpleasant an encounter with a guard myself.

We had been ordered on to the railway, to unload a trainload of logs. While working in my wagon, I observed another brigade, composed mainly of older men, trying to move a huge tree-trunk on a nearby wagon. They were unable to lift it so I went over to assist; but my brigadier saw me and ordered me back to my wagon. As I turned to go back, the brigadier in charge of the old man's brigade ran up behind me and struck me on the head. Because I had only been trying to help, I lost my temper and struck him back. When one of his colleagues approached, I tripped him so that he fell on the railway. There was a deathly hush. Everyone stopped their work, waiting to witness the outcome.

On such occasions we were generally ringed by guards who pointed their machine-guns towards us; one of the guards requested his officer for permission to shoot me. Fortunately, Antonos Bruzhas, who could speak Russian, was standing nearby, and immediately came to my rescue. He explained calmly to the officer what had happened, pointing out that I had been trying to help the old men, and had then only acted in self-defence. He said he knew me, and that I was not the sort of man to start a brawl. He added, and this for some reason impressed the prison authorities, that I had been on the staff of the allied forces during the war and had served with the British Army!

The officer asked if this was true. I said it was, and he ordered me to get back to my work. But that evening, the brigadier I had struck reported me to the camp authorities. These reputed offences were taken very seriously and I was sentenced to ten days in the *karker*. As it was summer, this was not unbearable, but I decided after the first day, to start a hunger strike. We found that this was a most effective device, because the Russians were, for some curious reason, nervous about hunger strikes. As they themselves were unable to resist food, or for that matter any of their animal or sexual urges, they thought that something very serious must be wrong with a prisoner who refused nourishment.

I was immediately taken before the camp doctor, a woman with the rank of captain. Helped by favourable reports from Miklos Csomos, who knew much more about medicine than she did, I was declared unfit for punishment and released.

Such incidents as this, whether I was personally involved or not, had a positive element; revealing the loyalty amongst prisoners. Had not Antonos and Miklos supported me at the risk of their own lives, I might well have lost my own.

Chapter 6

THE BANDITS

Bandits were present in force in Camp 10. They terrorised everyone including the guards. They frightened the canteen staff into giving them extra food, and the medical staff into providing codeine; this they took as a stupefiant, together with alcohol and morphia. There was no point in complaining, because they soon discovered who had informed on them and the "traitor" was likely to find himself with his throat cut or strangled in his sleep.

The first time I became aware of them was when the new chef in our canteen courageously decided to stop their traffic with the kitchen staff who gave them extra food, thereby reducing the other prisoners' rations. He paid dearly for this. One day we saw him being chased by two bandits towards the hospital, with blood streaming from his face and neck. He only just reached the door in time; there, he collapsed. The orderlies dragged him in before they could attack him again. They then tried to smash down the door; but the camp guards came running up, and the bandits had the effrontery to go off to the *karker* where they cynically asked to be taken in, saying the punishment for their act would be two weeks' detention.

The bandits were great gamblers. Cards were forbidden, but they ingeniously invented other games of chance. They would play during the night, and to avoid detection by the guards, would make little dummies from rags and old clothes, which they placed under the blankets on their beds. Not only did they gamble with their own possessions, but with those of others. They would gamble, for instance, as to who should rob an old man of a food parcel. The loser had to commit the crime. Sometimes a bandit who was not as heartless as his colleagues, would require narcotic stimulation beforehand. If they could not get camp drugs, they would make their own *chihar*, a highly concentrated form of tea. Tea, they obtained from the frightened canteen staff.

If a "traitor" in the camp was to be punished, the execution of his punishment was likewise decided by chance. On one occasion, the lot fell on a bandit chief named Mussa, an oil engineer from the Caucasian mountains who had a reputation for toughness, and who could be relied upon to execute the sentence. His skull had once been cracked and there was an opening in his head through which pulsating arteries were visible. The blow responsible for this had paralysed his left side; but the right was still very active.

This time the man to be punished was a Polish doctor who had refused to supply the bandits with drugs. Mussa wrapped half a brick in a cloth bag and made his way into the doctor's barrack block. He then stalked up behind him unobserved, and struck him on the head with the bag. The victim's skull was smashed and he died on the spot. Mussa then went to the authorities and reported that he had killed a Polish doctor.

As a matter of form, a court martial or trial was convened. It was held in the canteen, and we were ordered to attend. It was the most cynical trial I have ever witnessed. The camp authorities smiled, the prosecutor smiled, the accused smiled and the audience smiled. And yet these smiles were concerned with the death of a human being! Mussa's penalty for murder was for him to recommence twenty-five years' sentence.

The prestige of the bandit leaders was considerable. Frequently, if they told the brigadier of their working squad that they and their men refused to work for the next few days, they got away with it. Occasionally the camp authorities showed a sense of humour. On one occasion, a bandit chief told his men not to work, saying to the camp commandant, "After all, we've got twenty-five years ahead of us. There's time for everything, sir. Certainly for work!" The camp commandant thought this extremely funny and roared with laughter, slapping the bandit on the back.

I must add a word about the self-mutulated prisoners, most of whom were bandits or connected with them. They were the only men who were tough enough to stand the pain. They had tremendous will power and knew enough of the régime to realise that there was no other way of escaping slow and painful death thorough perpetual overwork.

Those who had mutulated themselves in our camp were a horrible sight. They came mostly from the ice-fields of the north, from Vorkuta, Petchora, Kolyma, and the other places with coal mines, where the work was hardest in Russia, and where railway lines connecting these places with the interior were being built by forced labour, under appalling conditions. Most of the self-mutilation took place in the years immediately after the war, when the ration and clothing situation was even worse. In parts of this northern Russian tundra area, the inhabitants lived in even greater poverty than the prisoners, and starvation took a heavy toll among the ordinary civilian population. We heard this from Russian prisoners whose parents were among the victims.

Self-mutilation was carried out either with dynamite,

or by making use of the new railways. A man would put his leg or arm on the rail and wait for the train. In winter, a method used was to place the limb on the line and urinate on it. This froze it to the rail in a matter of seconds, as well as rendering it insensitive to the shock; but many were so desperate that they could do it without even this primitive anaesthetic.

In our camp, prisoners without arms or legs were very poorly supplied with artificial limbs. A proper artificial limb was unknown and they used pieces of wood which they carved for themselves, attaching them to their stumps with string.

In theory, criminals were separatd from political prisoners and placed in their own camps. However, one wonders why we political prisoners found the mutilated bandits so often in our midst? The answer is simple and bureaucratic. By self-mutilation, a man sabotaged the labour system and therefore became, automatically, a political offender.

One of the strange features of bandit psychology was their attitude towards the West. Although these men were rebels against the anti-West Communist system, they regarded Western ideas almost with veneration. This explains why we Europeans were not molested. Indeed the bandits often helped us. As they knew how communism worked and we, at the beginning at least, were ignorant, they offered to protect us and warned us about the traps laid by the camp administration. They also informed us of the prisoners in front of whom it was dangerous to speak, the stool pigeons. They were quite ruthless with these men and considered it their duty towards the West to liquidate them. They were equally ruthless with any of their own circle who betrayed or deserted them, or disobeyed their orders.

However well-disposed the bandits might be to Westerners, they always maintained a closed shop attitude, carefully guarding their innermost secrets and seldom disclosed their thoughts or plans to outsiders. It was unusual and surprising to find such an efficiently organised body amongst the Russians, whom we Hungarians always looked upon as hopelessly inefficient.

Although a man was once murdered in the bunk above mine, my own relationship with the bandits was amiable. I was a European and therefore educated. In early days however, they stole my shoes, my pipe and the tobacco pouch which the Japanese engineer, Okano, had made for me out of a few silk rags. But Bruzhas had came to my rescue and had lectured the bandits into respecting my property. Perhaps because he had run a newspaper, he had a remarkable influence over these usually ruthless men and often succeeded in restraining them.

If a stool-pigeon suspected that the bandits might attack him, he would ask the authorities for a transfer. This was occasionally granted, but with the usual result. News of his transfer would reach his new destination by bandit bush-telegraph before his arrival. Sooner or later they took their revenge.

It was a long time before we discovered how the bush telegraph worked in this vast country, where there was almost no means of communication between towns, let along linking individuals. Some of the camp officials were former army officers who considered that they were now serving in inferior posts, and who were far from enthusiastic about the régime. These discontented camp officials, who naturally knew when a prisoner was being transferred to another camp, would inform the bandits. By their request, the information would then be forwarded through this channel to similar discontented camp officials in the new camp.

The most remarkable example of the bush telegraph's effectiveness was the way in which twenty-eight isolated mines in the Arctic Vorkuta region went to go on strike simultaneously.

Chapter 7

KALEIDOSCOPE OF NATIONS

I counted twenty-eight nationalities amongst the heterogeneous three thousand prisoners in Camp 10. Fourteen of these were European; others came from republics of the Soviet Union, but there were also Tibetans, Turks, Japanese, Lapps, Iranians and Eskimos. At mealtimes and proverkas, a babble of different tongues arose from every corner of the hall and parade ground.

Of these nationalities, the people who impressed me most were those of the Baltic States. Inhabitants of the three states on the eastern shore of the Baltic Sea, Lithuania, Estonia and Latvia, were until recently almost forgotten. It is an incorrect assertion to consider them as under-developed people living on the fringes of European civilisation. Indeed, I now discovered that their knowledge of life and literature surpassed that of other more favoured countries in Europe.

They were the first to welcome and assist newcomers who did not know their way about; they shared their food parcels, and claimed a particular kinship with the Hungarians, whose language and history they expressed an interest in learning. They told us how they, the Estonians, the Latvians, and the Lithuanians, who had not been the best of neighbours in the past, were now united against the common Russian enemy; that they had fought, and were still fighting, for their independence.

The Western world could do well to learn more about these brave people who have been resisting Russian Communism for almost five decades, a fight which has led to a drastic lowering of their population. Many, including elderly people or children, were deported to distant parts of the Soviet Union to make way for new settlers from Russia. In the Ukraine, Bukovina and Galicia, the Communists learnt that the best way to deal with guerrilla warfare was to cut the partisans off from their sources of supply and information, the towns and villages, by simply deporting their populations.

Many of the Baltic prisoners in our camp had not been captured as partisans; they had been arrested in towns and villages on trumped-up charges, generally for "collaborating with the fascists", which was ridiculous, for their people had fought the Germans as courageously as they now fought the Russians.

These hapless nations have learnt a hard lesson during their history; one of successive German and Russian occupations. A device they used against these two giant neighbours was their local shooting units, or clubs, which served as sports clubs in peace-time, but supplied skilled marksmen in time of war. To belong to these was now a criminal offence. But the Estonians and Latvians still had thousands of square kilometres of thick virgin forest, where the partisans dug themselves underground shelters, and where a very few still held out. It was not difficult to obtain ammunition, because the retreating German army had left large supplies behind them.

Later, in the spring of 1954, just before I was to leave Russia, an Estonian doctor arrived at our camp, and told me that he had been operating with a unit of twenty partisans in the forests for the previous eight years. When I expressed surprise that this guerilla war should still be going on, he informed me that fresh units were even then being formed in the forests. But their activities were becoming increasingly difficult because, with the arrival of alien and hostile Russian settlers, co-operation with the villagers was harder.

These Baltic prisoners were regarded as Russians by the camp authorities, and were therefore allowed to receive letters from their families. I wondered if this was really such a blessing as the letters always contained stories of family tragedies or of fresh deprivations and deportations. Some prisoners became demented when they received correspondence from members of their families who had been deported to unknown Siberia. Others worried about news from their elderly parents. We considered ourselves lucky that we did not have to undergo this particular form of torture. If one has to be permanently severed from one's family, it is better that the separation be complete and that one gives up all hope of ever again hearing from them. We were told of a young Estonian engineer whose wife, assuming that he was dead, married again. When she learnt that he was still living, she killed her two children and committed suicide. There were the two elderly Estonians too, who received news that their prisoner son had died; they set fire to their house and then committed suicide. But the report had been false. He was still alive.

These Baltic prisoners were the most homogeneous of the groups in Camp 10, except for the bandits whose homogenity was created by common nationality. They did not look to the West to freedom. They remembered its behaviour during the Russian Revolution, and again in Hitler's time. Although the League of Nations had recognised their sovereignty, no action had been taken for their benefit by the major powers. When the Russians occupied their nations after the war, the West could do nothing. Although the Baltic States were on the agenda of the various international conferences which took place after 1945, neither Messrs. Truman, Eden, Bevin, Mollet, nor the rest of the negotiators could make Russia relent over Latvia and Estonia. "We are the stepchildren of Europe", one of them said to me. However, I knew that Anthony Eden had done his utmost for them, and I tried to explain this.

Whenever the Western enthusiasts in the camp started talking about the West and how wonderful it must be to live there, of the impending Western liberation which would bring happiness to everyone, the Baltic prisoners attempted to disillusion them - not unpleasantly or bitterly, but simply by explaining that there was little hope as the West would never start a war on their account.

One Lithuanian with whom I made friends had been Lenin's chauffeur just after the Revolution. He had accompanied the Russian leader everywhere, had eaten at the same table with him, and had often slept in the same room. "We were happy in those days, with our new revolutionary freedom," he laughed. "I was young then. I was told, as were we all, that real life had just started. Freedom was round the corner. Lenin and his colleagues, I must say behaved very decently. He was kind and thoughtful to his subordinates. He would turn in his grave if he knew what happened afterwards in the Soviet Union. He was so different from the ones that followed. He was cultured, well-read, a real gentleman."

I pointed out that this "real gentleman" had started the dreadful revolution. He agreed that it had been a mistake from the start; that Lenin and his friends must bear a large part of the blame for the crimes which Stalin was later to commit.

The next most interesting racial group were the Poles, with their tragic history. As a result of their suffering, they proved better fitted than most to stand up to the hardship of life in a concentration camp. Some of them had had the harshest experiences, in the Vorkuta mines where summer lasts for only five or six weeks. In this extreme north of Russia there are no trees; the only vegetation is lichen, and even this is visible only for a short time in the summer. During the rest of the year, snow, ice and frost cover their country.

The district of Vorkuta, the Poles told me, has a large network of concentration camps; it produces the best anthracite in the U.S.S.R. These Poles were the first inmates of these camps. Prisoners had been taken during and after the Russian invasion of Poland in 1939 and deported, often by most primitive means, on sledges. For over ten years they had worked in the mines and on new railways, in the worst possible conditions. It was commonplace that, "under each sleeper of the railway to Vorkuta lies the body of a Polish soldier."

The supreme example of Polish bravery was revealed by a strike of Vorkuta miners in 1953. By then, they had reached such a state of desperation that they told their overseers that they would no longer labour in the mines and that they wished to go home immediately. This demand having been contemptuously refused, a young Polish ex-communist colonel organised the strike in Camp 29. Within two days, all the mines in the Vorkuta area had stopped working. No one knew how the news had been spread, for the mines were far apart in an almost uncharted region of Russia; there was no known means of communication between them. The coal supplies for the entire Leningrad industrial district which used mainly Vorkuta anthracite, were disrupted.

Soviet authorities were so put out by this strike that they sent the Attorney-General and the Vice-Minister of the Interior to investigate. The prisoners of Camp 29 were assembled on the parade ground. The Vice-Minister addressed them, asking them to state their requests. To their repeated demand to go home, he replied with one simple almost naive, question, "But who will work here, if you don't?"

It was true; only forced labour could be used in such a climate. If that was the Poles' demand, he refused to discuss the matter and told them to return to work. At this point all the prisoners left the parade ground. The Vice-Minister of the Interior and the Attorney-General of the U.S.S.R. were left standing alone in the middle!

For ten days, not a mine in the district was working. The authorities erected loud-speakers over the camp, and military music was played, interspersed with propaganda slogans and threats. Troops armed with machine-guns were brought and, on 1st August, it was announced that if there was not an immediate resumption of work, they would start shooting.

Nobody moved. A few minutes later, the machine-guns opened fire. A hail of bullets came in through the wooden walls of the barracks and within minutes two hundred and forty were wounded, and twenty-nine dead. Then came a pause in the firing, and further demands were heard over the loud-speakers. That was the end. In order to avoid further bloodshed, the Polish colonel ordered the prisoners back to work. The strike was over;

he and the ring-leaders were arrested and executed. This was confirmed to me in 1958 by a Hungarian veterinary surgeon, Gaspar Szep, who was in Vorkuta at the time.

Another group in this kaleidoscope of nations with which I became friendly because, as with the Austrians, their country was close to Hungary, were the Germans.

The older German prisoners still lived in a make-believe world of Kaiser Wilhelm II. Their happiest memories went back prior to 1914, and they talked of the "good old days". They blamed Hitler for their misery, claiming that he had upset the balance of Europe and had introduced the Russian bear for the first time in history.

Curiously opposed to them were the middle-aged Germans, most of whom had done well under the Dictator in the boom created by his war industry. They, too, could not forget the good life they had known in the "thirties," and reasoned in a peculiarly childish way. There was little point in arguing with them; their group contained a number of important Nazi officials including General Lombard, one of Hitler's Aides de Camp.

Lombard was an intelligent man, with a powerful personality; his influence on the younger Germans in camp was so great that there was a permanent rift between them and the other nationalities. We tried to play down these differences, for we did not want the Russian authorities to see the various groups of Westerners squabbling among themselves.

I worked beside General Lombard for two months, in the same brigade, loading tree-trunks; I even helped him at work, because he was in poor health and weaker than the others. What appalled me most about this Nazi fanatic was that he still annually celebrated Hitler's birthday.

He would save his bread ration for three weeks; then, with a few Nazi friends, he would celebrate the day with a bread orgy!

An irony of camp life was that General Lombard's bunk neighbour had been Lenin's official interpreter, another fanatic, but this time a Marxist fanatic. Although polically they were diametrically opposed, these men were able to forgive each other for their different ideologies; they even claimed to understand one another's points of view. But they could not forgive me for my Western liberal ideas.

Partly because of this, I could not resist bringing Lombard together with a Jewish prisoner, an old man whose family had suffered greatly under Nazi persecution. His eyes blazed when he learned who Lombard was; all he could say to him was "Look! Look! Just look what you Nazis did to us!" To which Lombard retorted automatically, "I'm sorry, but it was the law."

Lombard even tried to argue that the liquidation of the Jews, the extermination camps and gas chambers, was Allied propaganda. I gave up trying to discuss anything with this bigot.

The only Englishman I met during all my time in Russia was Alec Peters; he had been attached to the British military mission in Rumania. He was about to sail for home in 1946, with his family from the port of Constanza, when he was arrested. The Russians had politely asked him to come ashore "just for two minutes", in order to deal with customs formalities. These "two minutes" had so far lasted eight years. His family had sailed without him. He was quiet, dignified and courageous.

Then there were two American sergeants whose

effervescent good humour had helped to keep our spirits up. One of them said that what he regretted most was "the lack of baseball." He even offered to teach us "the best game in the world" when we returned to civilisation.

A bit more exotic, but equally representative, prisoner was a Spanish refugee from the Republican Army who, after fighting for the Communists in the Civil War, had fled to Russia, mainly by boat or over land through France. He had intended to seek asylum in what he believed was the home of socialism, but after a few months, he and his fellow idealists had found themselves behind barbed wire.

The French, Austrian, Dutch, and other European races who were our fellow-prisoners, are familiar to Western readers. But I must say a word about the multitude of races which make up the USSR itself, many of whom are as dissimilar among themselves as Latins, Anglo-Saxons and Teutons are to one another. From the region of the Caucasus alone I counted fifteen different races. There were innumerable peoples from the Urals, the Tartars in all their varieties and the local inhabitants of the Dubrov area, the Chuvashes and the Mordvinians.

We had an Estonian ethnographer among us who explained that we were now in the region in where our forefathers, and all the Finno-Ungrian peoples, spent a hundred and fifty years during their great migration from Asia, driven before the advancing Mongolians. When they reached Europe's frontiers they divided into two streams, the Finns and Estonians going north and the Hungarians south west. As a Hungarian, I was fascinated to meet Mordvinians, people who did not migrate as far as we and the Finns had. I often talked with members of these related people, attempting to discover affinities in our languages.

There were also Armenians, prisoners from Transcaucasia and Soviet Central Asia, Azerbajanees, Georgians, and men from Kazakhstan, Tadzhikistan, Uzbekistan, Turkmania and other territories, all of whom formed further racial groups. It was difficult to get to know them, partly because of language difficulties and partly because we could not fully appreciate their peculiar Eastern mysticism; partly too because, in our presence, they lacked self-confidence. They seemed happy enough among themselves, living their own secluded lives. Nearly all were Moslems, calm and disciplined, meticulously practising their rites and saying their prayers
regularly at daybreak and sundown, under the direction of their muezzins. The Soviet authorities unsuccessfully tried to discourage this. I learnt that their persistent devotion was to be found in all the camps of Russia. At first they did not know who we were and were suspicious, but the initial timidity diminished, and we later experienced the generosity of these half Asiatic people towards us Westerners. The same could be said of the Buddhists, with whom we quickly made friends.

There were a number of Tibetans, and a multitude of Far Eastern people. One of their lamas, a civilised man, skilled in ancient medical practices, tended the sick of every nation. He spoke French and introduced us to two Mongolians from Ulan-Ede, near Lake Baikal, who had been condemned to fifteen years' imprisonment for "incitement and propaganda." He remarked ironically that he could not imagine them inciting anyone; they were so uneducated that they could barely pronounce their own names. They had not been tried, but had been arbitrarily arrested and brought here.

The lama was touched when I pronounced the familiar incantation of his language, Omane padne hum. He made deep obeisances, embraced me, and even presented me with one of his few possessions, an old wooden Mongolian pipe. I treasured this for months, until it went the way of most personal possessions, stolen by the bandits.

Many groups of younger Soviet citizens had been brought up without religion, Eastern Ukrainians, White Russians and some of the Tartars. They lacked the moral fibre of the others; but they too, soon leaned to adapt themselves to the general atmosphere of the camp, to feel pity for the suffering. Subconsciously, they had adopted the Commandments: "Thou shalt not steal", "Thou shalt not kill", "Thou shalt love thy neighbour".

As well as religious and ethnological groups of Soviet people, there were also political distinctions. The old generation of Russians, including a number of officers, had served in the Tsar's army. Nearly all over seventy, they had been brought up as Christians. It was with these older Russians who spoke French and German, that we had most in common.

After them came the early Communists, now mostly in their late fifties, the first supporters of the 1917 revolution, who had believed fervently in Lenin and in the future of Communism. Disillusioned, they had learned during those terrible days in the thirties, that it was enough to declare oneself a follower of Lenin to be condemned without trial.

Within this group were sub-divisions: the old revolutionaries who still considered themselves good Socialists, declaring the Stalinists to be heretics and criminals who had besmirched the sacred name of Communism;

and a large group of older Communists who had simply become disillusioned with the whole movement, and who now no longer believed in anything. Having not been brought up as Christians and knowing no religion or philosophy save Communism, they wandered about in a mental void, and spoke bitterly against everyone and everything.

There was also a group of ex-Stalinists, former secret police or army officers, government officials and even ministers, who had become victims of personal intrigue, or sectarian quarrels; they too had been imprisoned without having seen the inside of a law court. A private report had been enough to imprison them; the large black car had come in the middle of the night, and their families had seen them no more.

Another Soviet group consisted of ordinary workers and peasants who had stolen government property, having not earned enough to support their families. They told us the new Russian proverb, "He who doesn't earn enough to live, steals the rest." There was not, they had to admit, much to steals, apart from a few pounds of flour, a sack or two of potatoes or some cabbage. They told us of mounds of corn, which, for lack of storage facilities, were left about in the open where moss grew on them, and they rotted. Yet, if they stole even one kilo of this they would be sentenced to fifteen years' imprisonment.

Finally, there was the large mass of rank and file Russian soldiers who had fought in the Second World War. In some ways, they were the saddest group. In the West, they had begun to appreciate the higher standard of living, the better working conditions, higher pay and other amenities which they had been taught were non existant outside Russia. When they returned to their villages after the war, relating what they had seen, they were sentenced for "spreading enemy propaganda". One soldier had told his friends that American Studebakers were more reliable than the Soviet Zis trucks. For this he was given fifteen years' hard labour.

Tragic too was the case of the Russian soldiers who had been sentenced simply because they had been taken prisoner by the Germans. They had been told to fight to the last, in the event of capture to commit suicide. One of them told me "I was separated from my family for four years. During that time we fighting soldiers did not receive letters or parcels from home - not to speak of leave. I was wounded three times. Instead of sending me home to recover, they sent me to the front to fight on - and bleed on - for the victory, the glorious victory of the Soviet Union. I was captured because I could hardly walk. Now at the end of the war, this is my reward".

Another Russian soldier had lost both his arms, was taken prisoner, and afterwards charged with treason for not having shot himself. "But how could I", he cried indignantly. "I had no hands to shoot with!" There was also another group who had contracted venereal disease in the West. They had been sentenced for sabotage!"

One soldier told me he could never forget what he had seen in Europe. "I now know it is to Europe that we belong," he said. "And if we fought again, it would be to establish contact with Europe, to join her community. I now know that everything we are taught here, the system under which we grew up, the perfection and superiority which we hear so much about, the things we fought for with such enthusiasm; it's a pack of lies."

Russian soldiers like this man soon found fellowship with the European prisoners, and became our friends.

Together with the bandits, who also knew the Soviet world, they often helped us in our problems with the camp authorities, particularly when we had to appear for interrogation. MGB officers would unexpectedly come in the middle of the night and question us individually, demanding information about the general mood of the camp, or about a particular prisoner. Sometimes they would ask for a deposition against a friend who was still in the West, on the basis of which he could be arrested or kidnapped. From these Russian friends we learnt the necessary duplicity, the way to reply, to tell our lies plausibly, and thus avoid causing disaster for those distant friends, and for ourselves.

Chapter 8

THE WOMEN'S CAMPS

Immediately after the war, there were several mixed sex camps in the Dubrov area. Later, men and women were separated; but the two sexes still often found themselves working together, mainly at technical rather than manual labour such as in the power stations, machine-workshops, hospitals and bakeries.

Normally men make advances, while women usually appear shy and disinterested. In our camp it was the reverse. Although biology may have played a role in this, there was another, more practical basis for this uterine frenzy. By giving birth in camp a woman could be sure of two years of comparative ease. As her child's "guardian" she did not have to work and remained in a maternity camp. As the state considered itself a kind of patron to these children, and attached great importance to their upbringing as future Communists, the mother received considerable material aid during the first two years. Immediately on attaining its second birthday, the child was snatched away from the mother and placed in a kindergarten. The pining mother resumed ordinary camp life, where she quickly searched for further sexual experience to initiate another pregnancy.

Sexual intercourse took place whenever possible; behind factory benches, in toilets, in the fields and above all, in hospital. This was a further reason why prisoners were always going sick. The younger ones, with their strong sexual urge, would do almost anything to get there, from feigning illness or poisoning themselves to swallowing needles, buttons, spoons, and in some cases deliberate mutilation. Once inside, discipline was not strict, because the prison doctors had their mistresses, and the camp administration did not wish to lose their few good medical men, upon whom the health of the whole camp, the guards included, depended.

One young German prisoner used to climb into the hospital and make love to a nurse in a bed in a private room. How he managed this princely luxury, I do not know. He was tall, blond, blue-eyed and good-looking. One day some nurses who had heard about his prowess, contrived to surreptitiously watch him. It was evidently such a masterly performance that they lost all self control, broke into the room, caught hold of him, and refused to let him go.

By now a number of other nurses had arrived on the scene. How could one man satisfy the craving of so many sex-starved women? One of the older nurses had heard that a piece of twine tied round the base of the male organ would keep it erect. This was done, and all the ladies were satisfied. I must add that the young man had to be carried back to his barracks on a stretcher. He never visited the hospital block again.

The palisades which divided men and women in the hospital quarters were not closely supervised. Anyone caught climbing over them generally received only minor punishment; but such was the sexual desire of some prisoners, that they would even dig trenches under the fences. It was not unusual for twenty men to have intercourse with one woman in the same night.

When the vigilance of the guards made it impossible for the men to reach the women, they contrived artificial insemination. The women would throw phials or small bottles, stolen from the ambulance or from the doctor's consulting room, over the palisade to a co-operative male. If a woman was found to be pregnant, she would receive only a small punishment; the Russians needed new citizens.

Prisoners who visited, or worked in the women's camps, told me they had seen embryonic bodies of babies in the toilets. Until a pregnancy is five or six months old, it is not visible and pregnant women had to continue working. Cramps and labour pains would suddenly come on, and the only relatively private place to which they could escape was the lavatory. Here they would have their miscarriages.

Abortion was less frequent, and then chiefly for women who had husbands and children at home, and who were serving sentences of less than five or six years. They hoped that, eventually, they would return to ordinary life, and were ashamed of having become pregnant through a chance encounter. But there were also unmarried girls who, during their early pregnancies, decided they did not want their babies; they too were ashamed, and often aborted themselves using primitive instruments.

It is strange how youth, even when overworked and under-nourished, knows no sexual barriers, and will go to any length to satisfy their biological urge. After 1953, when conditions improved, there were better rations, and the Red Cross food parcels began arriving from abroad, sexual craving became a mania, on one occasion causing a mutiny in the women's camp. They put down their spoons in the diningroom and started a hunger strike. This hunger strike for male partnership lasted for days. In chorus they shouted, "Bring us men! Men! Men!!!" Eventually, the commandant himself had to calm them. A humourless man, he only angered them with his bureaucratic jargon. "This is an ungrantable wish," he said. "According to the latest administrative orders of the Soviet Union the sexes are to be segregated. It is not within my jurisdiction to alter orders."

While he was saying this, one of the women, a prostitute, ran forward, tore off her clothes, and offered him her naked body. "If you can't provide us with proper men," she cried, "we'll have to make do with you, Commandant. Take me!"

Women prisoners often behaved more grossly than the men because many were blatnoi girls - particularly low types of Russian women, some of whom were ladies of the street. They were shameless, often as ruthless in satisfying their desires as the bandits. Many of them were real prostitutes whom, the Soviet authorities proudly announced, had been banished from the streets.

An embarrassing category of female prisoner was the prison barber, (women tended to take on the less strenuous services). Our beards and, as a precaution against lice, our bodies were shaved every week. This gave the blatnoi girl barbers countless opportunities for obscenities. I recall a young priest who became very embarrassed while his body was being shaved. "Don't worry, Father," she cried, "I'll do you well, but in return, I want to have you. You have such a good one!"

Sex life was different for the miners in the far north, such as in the Vorkuta mines. These prisoners had better treatment because their work was essential and they were so remote, being many thousands of miles from civilisation, and had no opportunity to escape. They had better food, and were even allowed to consort and visit the families of free Russians living in the neighbourhood. It was inevitable that sexual relationships should take place in such relative freedom, and many illegitimate children were born. After 1953, when the Soviet Union began to grant amnesties to foreigners, permitting them to return home, I heard of many Hungarian miners being accompanied by "partners in life" and their Russo-Hungarian children.

On one occasion during this repatriation period, a group of new prisoners arrived in our quarantine buildings. They were mostly Russians, but their was a Hungarian woman among them. In the evening, I waited for an opportunity to talk to her through the palisade.

She was beautiful, with an oval face and brown hair. She signalled to me as she approached the palisade and asked despairingly: "Are you Hungarian?" On hearing my voice, she clutched the bars and began weeping. She said she had not heard a word of Hungarian for six years. Her name was Countess Maria Szechenyi; she came from Eotvos Puszta, and was the daughter of Count Paul Szechenyi, a member of one of the oldest families in Hungary. We had many friends in common. Quite frequently, thanks to the help of an Estonian doctor, we were able to exchange letters and even meet. I came to know her quite well.

One day, an order came for her to move to another camp. I did not sleep that night and waited outside the departure building in the early hours of the morning. When she appeared, she told me she had been issued with dried food for five days, which generally meant a long journey east; she knew she was bound for Siberia. I tried to console her, telling her that she would probably be taken to Lvov, the repatriation camp, and that she would return to Hungary. I told her that, whatever happened, I would not forget her; I would trace her and not let her die. She made the sign of the Cross and left, crying desperately during those last minutes   Later I heard that her fears had been justified; she was deported to Siberia. When I complained to the camp authorities, I was told "Her aristocratic origins made her a particularly difficult case." What a way to describe banishment to one of the world's most notorious places.

The most brutal event I heard of during the whole of my time in the camps also occurred in hospital. It took place shortly after the war, in 1945 or 1946, when conditions were deplorable and prisoners were dying of hunger. The authorities employed free Russian personnel from outside the camp among whom was a female doctor. She was fat and well proportioned; one evening she was attacked by a group of famished prisoners, probably bandits, as she was returning home after work.

As the woman passed one of the barrack blocks, the prisoners grabbed her and pulled her inside. The barracks were built on piles, and between the floors and the ground, was an empty space. The woman was dragged into this and raped. But they had further interests. Such was their hunger that they killed her, chopped up her body and cooked it over a fire made of the loose planks. They ate her and burnt the bones.

Western prisoners who had heard about this did not wish to talk about it, but we were introduced to one who had unwittingly taken part in the revolting feast. He had been told he was eating dog meat, and the other prisoners advised us not to tell him the truth. Later, he did discover it and was sick for weeks.

Not all the sexual relations in the camp were

heterosexual. Some of the Westerners, Germans, Danes, Dutch, the so-called civilised nations practised homosexuality. This is generally alien to the Russians, Balts, Czechs and Slavs. Only once did I come across a Hungarian male couple. Homosexuality was easier to practise than heterosexual love, and the men who did so were quite shameless about it, sleeping together in their bunks, in the presence of us all. I remember a German pair in our barracks who had been together for three years. When they were separated and sent to different camps, they were in tears. We almost felt sorry for them.

Concentration camp life had many strange effects on the sexual behaviour of the inmates.

Chapter 9

SELF-MADE DOCTORS

A camp hospital was not only attractive for the sexual amenities it offered: we all wished to be there for a variety of other reasons.

When we were ill, a serious, if ineffective, attempt at diagnosis and cure was made; the hospital was divided into several sections, like any hospital in the west, for such as abdominal diseases, contagious diseases, surgery and dispensary. But the equipment was so primitive and the doctors and *feldshers* high category male nurses used as physicians in the Soviet Army and in rural areas, were so ignorant, that they were seldom effective. There could be no better proof of this than the delight of the camp authorities when a European doctor or dentist, like Miklos Csomos, arrived as a prisoner. He would be immediately seconded for hospital duties, where he would have no more faithful and devoted patients than the members of the camp administration, the MVD officers, their wives and their children.

Indeed, any camp possessing a West European doctor or dentist considered itself fortunate, because their knowledge was far superior to that of their Russian colleagues. There was always a processeion of free Soviet Citizens, Mordvinian peasants from outside the camp, in the corridors and waitingrooms of these well trained medics, who were also taken outside the camp under armed escort to perform operations on people in their homes. The West European doctor prisoners lived under rather better conditions than we did, but they had more work than they could perform, at all hours of the day and night. They often saw their patients die for lack of proper medical equipment and drugs.

In Tsarist times, good Russian doctors could be compared favourably with West European doctors. But after the Revolution, when thousands were liquidated with the rest of the bourgeoisie, fled abroad or were imprisoned, the medical system disintegrated. Russian doctors, having spent ten or fifteen years in a concentration camp, had been cut off from medical progress. Fully aware of this, they did their best to catch up. In some cases they succeeded, because their original training had been good.

One of the younger Russian doctors told me of the extraordinary examination system by which medical students qualify in Russia. At the end of the fourth year, they are divided into groups. Each group appears before a jury. This jury treats the students rather as a merchant treats a sample; he chooses one at random, examines it, and makes his decision whether to buy or not to buy. Similarly the jury picks out one or two students from the group, and asks them a few questions. They judge the level of medical knowledge of the whole group on the basis of the individual. If eighty students appear before a jury, some seven or eight are examined. If they pass, all eighty pass, if they fail, all eighty fail. Many of these young Soviet doctors were ashamed of their ignorance even, though they had worked hard at study.

The Western doctors considered it a duty, and often a pleasure, to teach them. Miklos Csomos held classes for them and the *feldshers* in the evenings.

The *feldshers* system, which is unknown in the West, dates from the Middle Ages, when the *feldsher*, a cross between a barber and a surgeon, cut, bled, operated and with luck, cured. The contemporary Soviet *feldsher* underwent a two-year course in nursing and medicine. Later, I understand, the course was extended to three years, but it was still superficial. Students were taught to give first aid and injections, to bandage wounds, nurse, prescribe simple medicines, and to diagnose the more common diseases.

Most of the hospital staff in Camp 10 were conscientious, well-meaning and humane. Even the most stony-hearted Russians were sooner or later moved by the suffering they saw about them. But there were unscrupulous *feldshers*, who levied taxes on the older and more helpless prisoners. To be satisfactorily nursed, these poor people had to pay a bribe, in the form of clothes, food, tobacco, or other private property. When the sick were moved from their barracks to the hospital, they brought their personal belongings in a sack which was kept in the hospital storerooms. These sacks were easy prey for the hyenas, as we called the bad *feldshers*, who divided the contents among themselves so that all became involved, no individual could betray the others.

The belongings of those who died in hospital were immediately appropriated by the hospital staff; just as the effects of those who died in the barracks were automatically inherited by the camp administration and the MVD officers. We often observed a pair of gloves, a scarf, or some other piece of clothing which had belonged to a dead friend being worn by the guards.

The camp pharmacy occupied one room in the hospital, and was run by a trained Russian pharmacist who was not a prisoner. In ours, two young free Russian Communist girls were employed as his assistants. Our doctor told us that they had to watch them very carefully to avoid mistakes as, though assistants were reasonably well trained, these two were very ignorant.

Fortunately, the pharmacist could not cause much harm because the drugs were of very poor quality and ineffective. But in the case of heart trouble, the size of the dose was important. Digitalis, for instance, is an excellent medicine, but its application requires precise knowledge. In our camp, the pharmacists distilled it from dried foxglove leaves, and the strength of the drug depended on how much they put in the water. At times, it was too strong while at others it was not potent enough; sometimes it did not act at all.

Western training was held in such esteem that it was enough if a prisoner had spent a year in a Western medical school, even if unqualifed, for him to be immediately appointed to an important position in the hospital. Once there, he stayed. As time progressed, the status of these medical men increased so that they were able to order their own drugs and medical books, and work on their own. So anxious were the authorities to employ Westerners with even the most rudimentary medical knowledge that some rather absurd situations arose.

A witty Hungarian friend of mine, forestry engineer Martin Schneider, told his brigadier that he could not work because he was ill. The brigadier took him to the *feldsher*, who asked him what was wrong.

"I have piles," retorted Schneider.

It was the only complaint he could think of which the *feldsher* might not care to examine. Unfortunately this *feldsher* was conscientious, and made him lower his trousers and bend over. He examined him and then declared Schneider to be a shirk; he had no piles.

"What! No piles!" said Schneider, "You're telling me. I, who am a doctor?"

The *feldsher* was taken aback. "You, a doctor!"

"Of course," Schneider unwisely replied.

"Wonderful! Marvellous! You don't know how good that is. We're terribly short of doctors. We've been hoping all along that some more European doctors would turn up and give us a hand."

The *feldsher* hurried to the camp administration. A few minutes later, Schneider found himself before the commandant who, after a few questions, ordered him to take over the convalescent wards, and undertake a nightly clinic.

Schneider was frightened; he said he didn't know whether to laugh or cry. Being a doctor was a responsible job, and he was afraid that he might cause the death of someone. He had had some first aid training with the army during the war, it was true, but that was years ago. They took him to the camp hospital and ordered him to work immediately that very night.

Among the older patients were a number of Hungarian officers; delighted at last to have a real Hungarian doctor to look after them. They hoped that this would make life easier, because doctors could do a great deal for their patients, not only as regards their health but also, most importantly, for their diet. Schneider decided to reveal the truth; he admitted that he was a forestry engineer, not a doctor. They were highly amused. He asked their advice.

"Keep on playing the doctor," they said. "However ignorant you are, you'll certainly do it better than these wretched *feldshers*!" If he was clever, they said, he could not only help himself by getting a soft job in the hospital, but also his recuperating fellow countrymen there. Being familiar with conditions in the hospital, they told him that a Hungarian with resourcefulness, daring and bluff could get away with almost anything.

After some misgivings, Schneider agreed. He possessed wit and daring and played his role to the best of his ability. He looked after his patients, obtained vitamin pills for them, and persuaded the camp administration to improve their food. Fortunately, he had a German male nurse working for him who had already spent two years in the camp, and who could recognise most common symptoms. He spoke and wrote Russian, and acted as Schneider's interpreter. Without him, Schneider would have been lost.

Before the war Schneider, a Hungarian of German extraction, had often visited Germany. During the war he had served with the German Army. Those experiences helped him now, because the interpreter trusted him, almost as one German would another. Schneider told him each situation as it occurred, and they organised the work accordingly. For some months they continued without a hitch, while Schneider learnt how to use the stethoscope, examine chests and rectums, and how to act like a qualified doctor.

One day Martin Schneider received a message that the chief medical officer of the Dubrov camps wanted to cross examine him. Schneider was terrified, but he still had a few days to study. He had made friends with a Lithuanian doctor who worked in another section of the hospital, to whom he also confessed his ignorance. This doctor had previously helped him solve anatomic and pharmaceutical problems. Schneider now studied with him so well that he was to come out of the examination with flying colours, and told to go back to his work.

All continued to go well until a new batch of prisoners arrived from the West, among whom was the chief assistant at the Department of Internal Diseases in the Berlin University Clinic. The camp administration, learning who this German was, immediately appointed him to the hospital, and ordered him to report to the chief medic, Dr. Schneider, under whom he was to work. The Berlin specialist said he would be delighted to work with a Hungarian doctor. He hurried off to the hospital to find Schneider.

Schneider turned red, then white, when he learnt the identity of the new prisoner. Again, he decided to tell the truth. He called the German into his office where he laid his cards on the table. The Berliner took the whole thing with good humour and told Schneider to stay where he was; they could work quite well together. He would examine the patients, and then tell Schneider how to treat them. In this way, they would be able to undertake even more for the patients than Schneider had been able before, when on his own. Schneider was not an unscrupulous man and would not have taken work from another doctor. There were simply no other doctors in the camp.

Schneider and his new "assistant" worked together admirably for a while, but his conscience started to trouble him, and he was constantly wondering how to extricate himself from the situation. He was also afraid of being found out. Finaly, he fell extremely ill, with pneumonia and pleurisy. There was no penicillin in the camp, and very few sulphonamides. It was fortunate that he was a "doctor" because, as a member of the hospital staff his trouble was soon diagnosed, and his colleagues were able to obtain extra food and medicine for him.

For a long time he hovered between life and death, but he eventually recovered. He then made the excuse that he was too weak to fulfil his duties as a physician, and left the hospital, to be transferred with a group of prisoners to the Vorkuta coal-mining region, where he worked as a machinist.

This was not the only case of its kind. In the Dubrov camp area, where I spent the greatest part of my captivity, there were lots of Germans and Hungarians who had never been physicians but who held medical positions; they too were clever and conscientious. Amongst these was my friend Istvan Szabo, who had been a medical student at Debrecen for a year until the war started; he then became an active officer in the Hungarian armoured corps. Captured at the siege of Budapest in 1945, he was taken to Russia where a military tribunal sentenced him to twenty-five years' imprisonment as a war criminal. Three years later he was brought to the Dubrov area.

He took his medical studies very seriously and found several well-trained Western physicians, who were only too glad to help him. They taught him and found him more useful and reliable than the Soviet *feldshers*, or even their physicians. In the eleven years he spent in Russian concentration camps, Szabo studied systematically, first from the extensive notes dictated to him by these doctors and second, in the last four or five years, from the medical books he was allowed to read. He worked in various hospitals, including the central hospital of the Dubrov area, and in the northern camp areas, as general practitioner, surgeon, and later as dermatologist. He even performed appendicectomies and rib resections.

When the Hungarian prisoners were sent back to Hungary, he accompanied them as their doctor. Yet he had never passed an exam in his life!

Another Hungarian, an airman, had no medical knowledge at all. When, by chance, he became a hospital nurse in Camp 9, he did so well that he soon became a head nurse, then section head, and was finally appointed medical examiner in charge of all autopsies. After 1950 the prisoners who died were taken to Camp 9 for autopsy. Previously, they had been buried on the spot, because the authorities were indifferent to the cause of
their death. Sometimes, he said, mysterious corpses were brought in from outside the camp by the MVD, or by army personnel who did not belong to the camp administration. They would swear my friend to secrecy, make him perform the autopsy, and then record his findings. He always knew when a body had been brought in from outside, partly because he would have recognised it had it been that of a fellow prisoner and partly because the most of them were shot in the nape of the neck, the standard Russian form of execution. He did his work efficiently, became an expert in anatomy, and it was only in the last years, on account of some love affair, that he was dismissed and sent back among the ordinary prisoners.

Another good Hungarian friend, Dr. Gyorgy Halasz, who was really an agronomist and had studied a little veterinary surgery, pretended to be a physician, and found himself one day doing his first autopsy. He was an intelligent young man, as skilful as Schneider in fooling the Soviets. This autopsy was on a man who had been beaten to death by the bandits. Because it was a camp murder, all the free medical officers of the camp area were present even though they made a prisoner do the dirty work.

Dissection for autopsy is always begun under the chin. Halasz, however, being ignorant, took the plunge and stuck his dissecting knife into the corpse's belly and cut open the bowels, so that their contents spattered all over the observers. He then cut the body in pieces as one might a dead animal. All the time he dictated his findings in German to his Estonian assistant. He used veterinary terms, not those used for humans, but behaved with such assurance that it did not occur to the Soviet doctors that he was an imposter. One of the Russian physicians even remarked quietly to another that it was very interesting to compare the difference between the Russian and the Western methods of dissection!

The best organised and most successful treatment in the concentration camps was surgery. When there was a shortage of medicines and drugs, there was a natural tendency to put faith in the scalpel. Our doctor friends and their patients told us about these operations, which were often performed without anaesthetic. Another friend, a Hungarian barber from Veszprem, suffered from stomach ulcers. One of these was perforated and an operation was necessary. He was taken to the central hospital where a Russian surgeon operated on him. This doctor was the chief of the surgical department, not a prisoner, but a free man. My friend told me that the operation lasted three hours without anaesthetics, and he was in terrible agony. But the Russian doctor reassured him, "Be patient, be brave, my friend, you are a Hungarian. Hungarians can stand anything, because you are the toughest fellows on earth." My friend told me how conscientious this doctor was. He had two operations to perform that night, but he did not go home between them and laid down on a bench in the corridor in preparation for the next. At other times, he would visit his patients almost hourly. Everyone spoke of him with gratitude and admiration. He belonged to the MVD, it was true, but he considered himself primarily a physician and surgeon.

There was another famous Moscow professor in the camp who, because of some intrigue, had been sentenced to ten years. He even performed brain operations. A throat specialist, an outstanding European doctor, performed a number of ear and mouth operations. There were some experts on nervous diseases, and a mental section for lunatics which was always overcrowded, for many of our unfortunate companions had gone out of their minds.

I must pay tribute to a Viennese physician of Ukrainian origin, Dr. Zderovich, who in his youth, had been assistant to the world famous Professor Chvostek, the founder of modern diagnostics at Vienna University. He was reputed to have performed miracles, not only on the prisoners, but also on the free workers outside. One night, he was taken to a woman with a perforated appendix and operated on her successfully by candlelight, using only a knife, in most unsanitary conditions. Zderovich was a wonderful man who will always be remembered with gratitude by thousands of prisoners. Thank God he was able to go back at his good work in Vienna.

As far as dentistry was concerned, there was only one treatment: extraction. Later, corruption, acting this time in favour of the prisoners, enabled the dentists to lay hands on one or two drugs and some drilling equipment. Those who had to be treated first were the MVD personnel, the civilian and military administration, and the free

Russians living outside the camp. Whenever a Western dentist like Miklos Csomos appeared, the camp authorities spared no efforts to obtain instruments for him.

As soon as Miklos arrived, he immediately set to work on the prisoners and found that many of the older men had lost most of their teeth. It was impossible in those first years to obtain false teeth; during my last year however, anyone with money could buy them, at least in the central and industrial camps. The camp administration turned this into a profitable private enterprise, demanding far more money for the false teeth than the cost of the raw materials, while the prisoners had to make them up for nothing.

In early Camp 10 days my own teeth came in handy in a very strange way. We had experienced another of the diarrhoea epidemics which periodically struck our camp, and were all feeling very weak. We needed cod liver oil and vitamins and had heard that one of the pharmacists, a free Russian girl named Komsomolka, had some to sell. As there was corruption in every walk of Soviet life, one could generally obtain anything if one paid.

Fortunately Miklos learnt that the Russian girl wanted a gold tooth, which she indicated that she would exchange for her cod liver oil. But where could the gold be found? We discussed the problem at length, and then I remembered that I possessed a gold crown on one of my back teeth. I suggested that Miklos might remove it. He tried but found it impossible to prise it away with his primitive instruments. I told him to extract the tooth. "God knows," I said, "how long we shall go on living on kasha. For that I don't need any teeth!"

Neither cocaine nor local anaesthetic existed, so I

gripped the arm of a chair and hoped for the best. A second later, the tooth was out. A new crown was hammered out in the metal workshop until it fitted the girl's tooth. The cod liver oil and vitamin tablets she exchanged in return cured a number of sick and elderly people.

There were two particular afflictions which gave the camp doctors almost insoluble problems, skin and venereal diseases. There was no dermatologist in the camp and no X-ray treatment; owing to the lack of vitamins in our diet, every variety of skin disease flourished unchecked. In the severe winters, this lack of vitamins caused many cases of scurvy and gingival atrophy. People lost their teeth, their nails became soft and their bodies were covered with sores. On one occasion, my entire body was covered with pustules.

Miklos Csomos could only look on helplessly at these skin diseases. He said that, although they were not in themselves dangerous, they could cause complications. Occasionally the authorities distributed vitamin pills, but three per head was all they could afford. On the advice of Miklos and his doctor colleagues, some of us decided to help ourselves as best we could, and substitute the deficiency of green vegetables in our diet with pine needles. They were evil tasting, but at least they contained vitamin C. After chewing these for some days the avitaminosis symptoms disappeared; I still have most of my teeth. Only three fell out while I was prisoner.

When we were sent out in the autumn and winter to clear the forests, and to fell trees, we would collect these pine needles. We would eat some and carry more back to our friends in the camp. It was not easy to smuggle anything as the guards made us turn out our pockets, and took away anything they found, imagining, I presume, that pine needles were weapons. During the summer, the problem was simpler, because we could devour grass and young leaves.

Many prisoners suffered from venereal diseases, particularly the more ignorant Russians from Central Asia who had taken part in the European War, where they had indulged in orgies of rape, unaware of the necessity to take precautions. Some had syphilis in its secondary or tertiary stage, with open sores. Usually the disease was only discovered at this point, because the victims had not realised with what they were afflicted, or had been too ashamed to report it. They lived for months among us, sharing our bunks, baths, even using the same half-washed underwear.

When they realised what their ailment was, they usually reported it, partly to go to hospital, partly to be exempted from work. Their treatment was inadequate, as most of the proper medicines were not available, or in short supply. They could only have a few injections, whereas dozens would have been necessary. This meant that the symptoms disappeared, but the disease persisted. Later, syphilitic patients were isolated in a special barrack block.

Until 1950, prisoners who died were buried naked in unmarked graves; the clothes had been confiscated. But, later, when the government needed proof that they had treated these many slave labourers with "humane consideration", and had given them proper hospital treatement, the camp authorities were ordered to decently bury them in graves. In my time, the dead were placed naked in plain wooden coffins filled with straw. Later, they were dressed in some underclothing, a torn shirt or underpants. The graveyard was outside the camp, wherever possible in a wooded or bush-covered area. A piece of board was erected above the grave with the prisoner's registration number, but never his name.

Before 1950 there were no autopsies, partly due to high mortality, partly because of the inhumane attitude adopted towards slave labour. We heard from some of the prison doctors, and the ex-MVD men imprisoned with us, that in those days the corpses were handed over to an MVD detachment, who took them away in a truck. The burial was performed by the so-called semi-free labourers who lived outside the camp; a category of half-prisoners, half-freemen, that then existed. Their orders were to pierce the chest with an iron spike, not only to prevent anyone from being buried alive, but also to prevent escape. This practice was eventually stopped. Instead, the skull was crushed with a heavy wooden hammer and they began disecting the bodies to discover which epidemics were the most virulent.

Chapter 10

FORESTRY PUNISHMENT

Early in the winter of 1949, "selectors" arrived to choose skilled and experienced workers for the industrial camps. To us they were slave traders.

Prisoners were divided into four categories and registered according to physical fitness. General Sergienko, commandant of the Dubrov camp system, addressed us and announced that the period of acclimatisation was over. It was now time for productive work.

The period of acclimatisation to which he referred had served his interests. It had given him and the slave traders time to catalogue the new prisoners according to reliability, potential danger to the regime and work capacity. We were probably granted this period to help us lose the initial feeling of vehement hatred which can cause rebellion.

Of the four grades, No. 1 was for the fittest who were transferred to the mines in other parts of the nation. Grade 2 was for men who were strong enough to undertake prolonged heavy work. Most in these first two categories were young, under thirty and even sometimes under twenty. Grade 3 consisted of men fit only for light work; while Grade 4 consisted of the elderly and invalid, unfit for any work.

My physical condition was poor, so I was placed in Grade 3. Nevertheless, anyone who had the use of his arms and legs was expected to work beyond his physical capabilities. That many prisoners collapsed and died at work from heart failure, or with cerebral haemorrhage confirmed this.

At last the day of our departure from Camp 10, 15th December 1949, arrived. Still in the rags I had been forced to wear for the last two and a half years, I stood with my companions knee-deep in the snow. We were surrounded by detachments of MVD men in huge sheepskin coats, fur caps and heavy felt boots. Russian political police like the Gestapo, their equivalent in Germany, were granted all the creature comforts; they were better clothed even than the Regular Army itself. The temperature was thirty-five degrees below zero centigrade; but before climbing into open wagons, we had to stand for over an hour while our personal data were checked for the hundredth time. Frost-bite took its toll and some of my fellow prisoners had to be taken to hospital when we arrived at our destination.

The MVD guards had several Alsatians and while we waited, they amused themselves by letting them loose and encouraging them to snap at us. This was to intimidate us.

We were transferred to Camp 11, which housed the general staff and central administration for the entire Dubrov camp area. Although it was only thirty kilometres away, we travelled by wagon for over two hours before finishing the journey on foot.

The area surrounding the new camp included the first Russian provincial settlement I had ever seen. One might, I suppose, have called it a town, but it was unlike any I had previously known. Only in the illustrations of Fennimore Cooper's Red Indian tales which I read as a child, had I seen such a collection of primitive log huts and neglected clap-board buildings.

We were now in the centre of a large timber-production region, surrounded by marshes and vast forests of oak, beech and birch, many of them hundreds of years old. The birches, not the variety we had known in Europe, were enormous. Two men could barely have put their arms around the trunk and touched the tips of their fingers.

We were marched through the picturesque little wooden settlement, in which only the military barracks and administration buildings appeared to be of brick. The other solid building was the radio tower, for no expense was spared on anything connected with "security." These, and a large industrial plant extending over several square miles, were surrounded by barbed wire and high palisades.

We marched to the factory where we were received by a MVD possé who immediately searched us from top to toe. Our personal data was again checked, an inevitable administrative procedure. I must confess that on this occasion, I was surprised at their efficiency; they had retained all my documents.

We were escorted to our barrack block. For lack of space, I was put with the Estonian group into the *karker*, which was larger than that in Camp 10. As there were plenty of young people and workers in this camp, there was more opportunity for "sabotage". This accounted for the larger *karker*. These *karkers* were of different kinds. In newly built camps, thy were not underground as in our camp; some were even heated. There was a slight improvement too in this stock camp punishment in later years, especially after the deaths of Stalin and Beria. It may have been the result of international protest, or perhaps on account of the adption of more humanitarian ways. But the improvement was so slight as to make very little difference to our lives.

We were kept in quarantine for a week, during which we met the brigadiers, the foremen and camp administrators, a veritable army of boot-lickers, who bullied us interminably. We seemed to have landed in a new unknown, where the ruthlessness of our slavery would be even worse than before, to gradually slide lower and lower down the slope of misfortune.

No sooner had we settled in than I began to suffer the consequences of my retaliation against the brigadier in Camp 10. This officer had also been transferred with us to Camp 11, and now told his new colleagues about me. Two of my friends overheard him describing me to Rogatshev, one of the most brutal brigadiers in the camp. He informed him not only that I had "attacked" him, but that I was a "dangerous fascist" who had murdered quantities of Russian and European democrats.

Rogatshev evidently intended to stamp his mark on us, for the next morning he called me out of the ranks by name and began cursing me as a "fascist beast and antisocial element." My brigade became apprehensive at this outburst, but the tough young Lett, my friend Harry Anderson, spoke up in Russian and told Rogatshev to take care because I was well liked and respected; I was not a fascist. "Rupert is very weak," he protested. "He should be given light work. The least you can do is to show him some humanity..." I was particularly grateful for this defence as I could not speak Russian myself.

The brigadier began cursing louder, accusing Harry of being a fascist too. "It's lucky for you that you've only got one leg, or we'd make short work of you!"

Harry again answered back, telling the brigadier that if he continued like this, he would not remain alive for long; we had powerful friends in the camp, he said, referring to the bandits. This sobered Rogatshev, for he stopped cursing, but he later muttered that he would make an example of us. The "example" I soon discovered, was to be me.

That evening, I was led to the stock-room where, with a number of old men, I was issued with warm clothing. I suspected what this meant, a punishment night shift in the open with a temperature forty degrees below zero.

When our companions had gone to bed, we were taken out to a railway siding and ordered to unload tree-trunks, oak, beech and birch, six metres long and often more than a metre in diameter. Such work was normally done by the fittest younger prisoners, and then only in daylight. But we were all ill and one old Ukrainian over seventy. Eighty of us had to unload thirty wagons. We worked from eight o'clock at night until seven in the morning; unloading by hand, as there were no cranes.

Within an hour, two men had broken their arms and another his ribs. One of the old men slipped when a huge trunk rolled towards him, and failed to jump aside in time. It crushed him and he died almost immediately. An old Ukrianian knelt beside him in the snow, crossed himself and began praying aloud. The brigadier and his assistants ran up and kicked the kneeling man, ordering him to get up.

We continued working like this; often during that night I heard old men crying, "*Bozhe Moi! Bozhe Moi!*" (Oh God! Oh God!) Younger prisoners were filled with such pity that we forgot our own suffereings, and went over to help them. Only at midnight were we permitted a few minutes rest, in the locomotive shed; when we came out we were greeted by a snowstorm. At the end of this night's work our ears, noses and hands had turned white with frostbite.

The next morning the bell sounded for roll call and although we had worked all night, we had to attend in the snow, standing for over an hour, while lists were consulted and numbers checked. The recollection of that first month in Camp 11 will remain with me for ever. I still shudder at it.

This punishment brigade in which I worked for three months, killed fifteen of its eighty members. Some died of accidents, some of pleurisy, and others of heart failure. They were given no medical aid, but even if there had been any, it could hardly have saved these old people in such conditions. Fortunately troups of younger prisoners arrived in February and took over the work.

Timber production was one of the most important industries in the region; it must have become obvious to the authorities that the elderly and sick were incapable of handling heavy material. Thus, this first dreadful period drew to a close.

After several further fairly heavy jobs in the lumber mill, where we had to break up ice-bound ground and lay foundations for houses, I found myself, thanks again to Harry Anderson, working beside him in the carpentry shop. This one-legged ex-S.S. Sergeant who had been previously forced into the Latvian Secret Service by the Germans, seemed to have influence in the camp, even with the authorities. The work, although strenuous, was at least indoors.

In the carpentry shop, I was introduced to the infamous Communist norm system. The obligatory minimum, or norm, was determined by factory management, often twenty-five per cent more than in civilian factories. When I commenced work in the carpentry shop, the daily norm for one worker was the upholstering of fifteen chairs. We received the frames, into which we fitted the square upholstered pieces for the seats, and oblong ones for the backs. All the work was done by hand, and we boiled our own glue. A few weeks after my arrival, the norm was raised to twenty chairs a day. By the end of the third month, it was thirty-five. This was no longer work, but acrobatics.

The logic which dictated these increased norms was most ingenious. Any output above the norm was rewarded with extra food. Those who achieved more than a hundred and ten per cent, received an extra fifty grammes of mush in the evening; those who produced over a hundred and twenty per cent, two hundred grammes of mush and twenty grammes of extra bread, and so on.

Understandably some prisoners, particularly the younger ones who were always hungry, tried to produce more and more chairs. In vain, we explained to them that this over-production required more energy, which could not be replaced by the relatively small quantities of extra food. Nor did they listen when we suggested that they should not serve the Soviet Union so well. Their empty stomachs had robbed them of their reasoning.

Faced with an avalance of chairs, the administration took the obvious course. "All right," they said, "if you can produce chairs so easily, we'll raise the norm by thirty per cent. You have obviously been idling. This is nearer your true figure."

The achievement of the few became the rule of all. This was particularly hard on the old prisoners, who could not keep up with the others. They knew that failure would result in transfer to work outside such as felling tress and loading and unloading wagons. To avoid this, some of them worked till they collapsed.

Thus the authorities had the means for compelling prisoners to exert superhuman energy. If this still did not do the trick, the "idle ones" were confined to the cold *karker* in their underwear. Here, sometimes these wretched men had to punch and beat each other, simply to keep their blood circulating. Many died.

It will be appreciated that I had every reason for working hard at my chairs, struggling against this nightmarish arithmetical progression. The manager of our carpentry shop was an exceptionally disagreeable women, who had graduated from the propaganda department, and had been for some time Party Secretary in the local village. Many of the factory managers, the so-called free Russians, were zealous party women, often more ruthless than the men. This woman drove us at a furious pace, denying us even so much as a whisper with our neighbours while we worked. She was a norm maniac, besotted with expanding percentages.

One day this hawk-faced female went too far. An old Estonian, whom she was reprimanding, picked up the chair on which he was working and crowned her on the head with it: he served a long spell in the icy karker for his action.*

---

* This courageous old man had once been a *Waldbruder*, or partisan of the Estonian woods. When he and his comrades had been finally cornered, he had shot two MVD officers, and fled with his machine gun to a near by village. There he waited until the MVD personnel were at dinner in their Headquarters he then entered and coolly fired several bursts as they sat at their meal, killing some fifteen before he was captured. Luckily for him, at the time the death sentence had been abolished.

In this camp there was a great deal of enmity between the various national groups with constant fights between Russians and Turks, Poles and Ukrainians, the bandits and the Caucasians. During my time three men were stabbed and one had his head severed. An old White Russian refused to hand over his mahorka cigarette to a young Caucasian bandit; the bandit simply picked up an axe and attempted to decapitate him. I once noticed in the workshop that a group of young prisoners were surreptitiously sharpening their knives during the lunch break. When I asked why, they replied that the knives had been ordered by the bandits and would be smuggled out to them in the food. Somehow the bandits always seemed to be able to obtain weaponry.

There were twelve hundred workers in the Camp 11 factory, and three hundred and twenty administrators, about eighty being free Russians; the other administrators were prisoners selected for their knowledge of book-keeping. Each workshop had its head and assistant book-keepers, working under such quantities of controls, checks and counter-checks that it was surprising that anything was produced. The inefficiency was redeemed by increased norms, by taking risks, and by ignoring all safety precautions. Human life was cheap, and replacements could always be found if any slaves were killed in a factory accident.

Most of the equipment had been confiscated as war reparations from Western countries where the Russian Army had fought. Some was modern, but the camp authorities did not know how to use it. The furniture factory where I worked was equipped with good rotary saws and planing machines, but there were no trained operators. After three days' training, prisoners were expected to use equipment which, in the West, would have required a minimum of three weeks' apprenticeship. The older, less nourished prisoners grew tired and lost their power of concentration; their reflexes were slow, and they were unable to make full use of the circular saw. One often saw men running for first aid, their fingers or hands dripping blood.

The saws revolved at three thousand revolutions a minute, but there was no automatic brake or screen. Sometimes, a piece of oak would split, and a splinter would be shot off with the force of a bullet. In one case, a splinter removed half the back of a man's head, and continued to penetrate a wooden wall behind. In another, the tooth of a circular saw broke off, and hit an operator in the forehead, coming out through the back of his head. We hardly realised what had happened before he suddenly collapsed and died, spattering everybody with blood.

A power station produced electricity not only for the camp, but for the entire MVD village outside. It had been built in 1923 and was very primitive. The cables had been laid without safety precautions, so that workers were continually getting electric shocks, some of them fatal.

In some woodwork shops, central heating had been installed, not for the benefit of the workers, but because heat was necessary for drying and varnishing the wood. Steam was chanelled by underground pipes to the workshops from the power plant, which contained a giant boiler. These pipes were also poorly laid and there were constant explosions; people were perpetually being scalded.

I continued working in the carpenters' shop until one May morning, I was summoned before the *oper*, the camp MVD officer. These summonings were not unusual for prisoners considered politically dangerous. By frequent questioning, the authorities hoped to involve more and more of our friends in the West. As I had suspected, this time it was in connection with the woman who managed the chairmaking. She had ordered me to produce five additional chairs a day, which meant a further daily two hours' work. I had asked her the norm. "I want to know," I said, "because you are entitled to ask me to fulfil the norm. But no more."

She went scarlet with rage and snarled that she would show me who was master. The *oper* told me that as a result of her complaint and of my earlier trouble with the brigadier, I was to be transferred to Brigade 72, the most notorious of the punitive brigades.

Members of Brigade 72 lived in a special barrack block which they were forbidden to leave, and they were not permitted to talk to the other prisoners. Their work place was far removed from those of the others, and they were supervised by a special military detachment from whom they even had to ask permission to go to the latrine. In spite of this, I managed to communicate by signs and messages with Antonos Bruzhas who would wave to me as I went to work. "Keep smiling!" I remember him shouting. "We'll soon get together again somehow." He even managed to smuggle me some tobacco. The Englishman, Alec Peters, was also in this Brigade. We were known as the "two bloody British spies".

My task in this brigade was to dig up large tree stumps with their roots, and carry them across the marshes to the sawmill. The camp was built on marshland; we sank into the peat at every step, under the weight of these stumps. There were many accidents; the stumps, some weighing half a ton, rolled on to the prisoners and crushed them. During my first week, fifteen prisoners had been conveyed to hospital.

One morning my group which was not very adept, dropped our tree which rolled directly towards me, knocking me down and striking the back of my head. I was lucky that my head had not been crushed. This happened at noon on a midsummer day, when we were working in the burning sun. Blood appeared before my eyes. My nose bgan to bleed, and when I attempted to rise, I stumbled and lost consciousness.

When I recovered, I had lost all muscular power; I could not move my legs or arms and lay half conscious, blinded in one eye. My Ukrainian fellow workers immediately ran to the guards, who sent for a *feldsher*. The *feldsher* examined me, saw that I was paralysed and unable to walk, and said that I must be carried to the infirmary. He asked the other prisoners to hoist me on his back, and he himself then carried me to the guard hut, five hundred metres away. Here I fainted again.

For two days, I remained unconscious. When I recovered I found that my right side was paralysed; I could neither move my arm nor leg. My lips were drawn to the right, and when I tried to drink water, it trickled out of the corners of my mouth. The doctor in charge of my case was very different from the *feldsher*. He accused me of shamming and to test my reflexes began scratching and cutting the skin on the sole of my right foot until it bled.

I was kept in the infirmary for three weeks, until I could move my limbs a little. But it was another two months before I could stand, and then only with crutches, because my right leg had lost the use of its muscles. Dr.

Suba, a Hungarian physician friend, advised me to pretend that I was paralysed. "If you show you can move your right side at all," he said, "they'll send you back to the Punitive Brigade, as 'cured'. That blow caused bleeding under your skull and you've had a cerebral haemorrhage. You'll die if you go back to work."

He gave me a penknife and recommended that, in order to foil the Russian doctor, I scratch the soles of my feet and the skin of my belly regularly until they bled. I carefully practiced not wincing, and succeded in misleading the doctor, who eventually pronounced me as Grade 4. I was then transferred to Camp 14.

Chapter 11

IN A FACTORY

On arrival in Camp 14, I was given another medical examination. The Russian doctor here was a kind of Devil's Advocate in reverse, interested only in the health of a prisoner's physique. He wanted to upgrade me; but the chief physician, who had been disabled in the war, took one look at me and told him not to waste time. He endorsed my three month's period in Grade 4.

Although this absolved me from productive work, I still had plenty to do in the routine cleaning of the camp, in the kitchens, raking and cleaning the sand strip between the wire fences and cleaning the palisades. Two brigades of cripples were employed all day, fetching water from the well for the kitchen and the bakery. But these three months at least gave me a respite, a chance to participate in some sort of social life, even to develop my interests. I had always wanted to improve my English, and here I had the opportunity.

I made friends with some elderly English speaking Russian prisoners who had lived for years in Shanghai. They had unwisely returned to their homeland in the twenties, hoping to find a "socialist paradise". It was a problem to obtain writing materials. At first we wrote in the sand, with a stick or with our fingers, ten or twelve words which we would learn by heart. Later, we inscribed wooden slates made from the bark of trees with pieces of coal. Finally, we acquired from the Camp Cultural Centre (such a place really existed in Camp 14!) one or two small stubs of pencil. Prisoners would steal them or barter them for pieces of bread. About twenty of us would then share one small stub. Along with our writings we hid these in cracks under the barrack floors, or beneath clumps of grass which we dug up with our hands. We were later able to use the paper which the book-keepers used in their offices. No white paper was available in Russia; account books were made of packing paper.

Continuing our intellectual pursuits, we formed little groups, each specialising in its own subject. I gave lectures to Rumanians and Balts on Central European history, law, economics, and literature. Although our knowledge was limited, the *linqua franca* was English. It was amusing to hear a provincial Hungarian speaking English to an Estonian gardener, or a Latvian sailor discussing Byron in English with a Polish cobbler. One of our friends, a Rumanian journalist, had been the Bucharest correspondent of the *Daily Mail* before the war. He had a good memory, and when we managed to steal packing paper from the book-keeping offices, he would write out excerpts from English novels or short stories that he had memorised. I recall with pleasure Somerset Maugham's '*The Letter*', part of which he could recite by heart. He would also write essays in English about the flora and fauna of his own country, particularly the Danube delta. He described his beautiful homeland so graphically that his English essays were among our most treasured possessions; they went from hand to hand, and everyone learned a part. I also made friends with a Lithuanian poet, Mishkinis. Although he had never been to England, he spoke excellent English, and gave a series of lectures on Byron and Keats. Mishkinis was one of the best known of his country's poets.

All this was very pleasant, but it was also dangerous.

Discovery meant sentence to several days in the *karker*, or expulsion from the tailoring factory to be put on outdoor work.

After three months, I was upgraded to Grade 3, and again put to work. As it was mid-winter, I had hoped to get into a factory, but there were too many old men who had to be given the indoor jobs; I was put in a brigade erecting and repairing houses.

It was unwise to build new houses in winter in the Dubrov marshland, because when the summer came the heat thawed and softened the frozen soil, and the buildings toppled. I remember seeing small bridges which we had constructed in winter, become lopsided in the warm weather. And yet we were made to build continually, because houses last only five years in this climate; they then rot and have to be replaced. We used oak or beech stakes for foundations; first we charred them, then sunk them in the soil as piles.

While repairing buildings outside the camp, I had an opportunity of seeing the home life of the MVD officials and officers. They were the privileged class in Russia, and one might have expected their houses to possess bourgeois amenities. But most of the interiors I saw revealed nothing but dirt, stench and incredible poverty. Their owners had no proper furniture, so they sat on boxes. Sometimes they slept on wooden or iron camp beds; more often, their beds were formed by two wooden trestles, linked by a blanket-covered plank. There were no carpets or linoleum, and the floors were unswept. Pots and pans were non existant and the cooking was done in tins. For glasses, they used aluminium or earthenware mugs. Later, when they heard that there was an Austrian turner in the camp, they obtained wooden mugs from him. They spat on the floor, and in the winter, if they felt it was too cold to go to the latrine, they ripped up a floorboard and relieved themselves in their own rooms. In summer the stench was unbearable. We prisoners hated them most for this; we had to clear it up. If there were plenty of fleas and bed bugs in our prison quarters, there were more in the houses of the officials and free Russians who lived outside. In fact, one of the MVD officers told me that he would prefer to live with us in the camp ... because it was so clean!

After several unsuccessful attempts to be allocated a factory job, I was lucky in the spring. I joined the clothing factory, thanks to one of the section managers, a Hungarian tailor, who asked for me although he knew I was untrained. His staff was almost exclusively European; the work required intelligence and accuracy. The norm was, as usual, ridiculously high, but I was delighted to see how my colleagues' ingenuity overcame this. Sometimes the factory would stop for days, even weeks, because of a lack of raw materials or spare parts. This they generally engineered themselves.

In Socialist nation-wide planning, the lack of one type of button, a hook, or an irreplacable needle, brings production to a standstill. On one occasion, the neighbouring furniture factory ran out of glue, and it stopped for ten days. Another time, a small wooden nail caused a standstill for a day. The sewing machines were attached to a single transmission belt, so that if this was out of order, all the machines stopped. We learned various ways of damaging this belt, and poured sand into the lubricating oil. To see some of the excellent British diesel engines, which had been commandeered in Czechoslovakia as reparation at the end of the war, break down as a result of our own sabotage was heartrending. But we overcame our scruples, and generally had at least one machine out of action.

Another difficulty which we aggravated, but which the authorities really brought upon themselves, was a lack of stock items such as wool, linings, cottonwool and padding. I heard later from a Russian textile expert that this was a deliberate part of Soviet industrial policy. To accumulate material, more at least than was needed for two or three days' work, was "sabotage"; because "raw material was lying unused"! We used about fifteen thousand yards of wool lining every day in the tailor's shop, and it arrived, or was supposed to arrive, daily. It was still damp when it came, having just been taken off the looms; it had not dried properly, and as it dried in our shop, it shrank. The shrinkage of fifteen thousand meters was considerable; this was most convenient, because stolen material could be attributed to "shrinkage". Everyone stole lining - the prisoners, the free workers, the guards, the manager. Yet, at the half-yearly stocktaking, the vast quantity of missing material was listed as "shrunken stock." Russian engineers and business-men told me that wherever political prisoners were employed in factories, it was the same; there was sabotage and pilfering.

The fundamental reason for all these troubles was the rotten industrial system. The Soviet Union was over-centralised, economically as well as politically. Everything was planned and calculated at headquarters situated thousands of miles away; everything arrived late because communications, which centralised planning demands, were poor. Not until Khrushchev came to power, was any attempt made to remedy this. A Russian industrial expert, now a prisoner, explained this to me one evening.

"But," I argued, "the Russian forces looted half Europe. They dismantled thousands of factories and stole some first-class machinery. I saw it myself. At the Egyesult Izzo factory in Budapest, for instance."

"Yes," he said, "we dismantled and took away everything we could lay hands on, it is true. But we have not really profited from it. What did not fall to pieces on the way to Russia, was ruined later. The distribution of all the machinery taken after the war was not organised. The greater part of it was left in the open, exposed to snow and frost, to rust and disintegrate."

A Carpathian teacher told me about a modern paper mill which had been dismantled by the Russians in Austria, and its machinery transported through Hungary as far as Raho in the Carpathian mountains. He said he had seen these machines thrown out on a siding in Raho. That was in 1945. He was then kidnapped, and sentenced to three years imprisonment in Russia for some trumped up crime. In 1948, when the sentence was over, and he was returning through Raho, he saw the same machinery, now rusty and still scattered where it had been left along the railway line.

The tailor's factory was a great advertisement for Singer sewing machines; some of them were 1920 models. Old and battered as they were, they still ran. How they worked! When our norms went up, the sewing machines had to work harder too. The revolutions are, I understand, not supposed to exceed fifteen to eighteen hundred a minute. But our Singer machines ran at two thousand five hundred, or even three thousand revolutions. The needles jogged frenziedly up and down, and sometimes the material under them smoked.

While working here, I met a Russian with the Anglicised name of James Bragin; he had been educated at Edinburgh University. His admiration for Britain was boundless, and he had deliberately changed his name so that it could be pronounced in an English way. When he heard that I worked for the British in Vienna, he became ecstatic and would hardly speak to anyone else. Poor man; his Anglo-mania landed him in jail.

Before the war he had worked in Archangel with a timber exporting firm, which had enabled him to keep up his connections with Britain. When the war came, he was sent to the Caucasus; here he saw Mrs. Churchill while she was visiting Russia on behalf of the Red Cross in 1943. As her car passed along the road, surrounded by a jubilant crowd, he became immensely excited and shouted,
"How glad we are that you have come, Madam! How grateful we are to you British! Welcome to our country!"

Although his countrymen were surprised that his English was so good, Britain was then an ally, and no one could take exception, officially. But the authorities were vigilant; they had noted his words. After the war, he was interrogated. What were his British connections? He told me that he had often spoken to friends in private about his love of Great Britain. He later discovered that almost every word he had said had been recorded. This, together with his friendly salutation to Mrs. Churchill, was enough to brand him as a "saboteur disseminating enemy propaganda." He had been sentenced to fifteen years hard labour.

Although he was aged sixty-eight, we became intimate, almost like father and son; a friendship which continued until his death in 1953, when his case was being reinvestigated. He was granted amnesty, but the poor man died two weeks before he could be freed. He was never reunited with his wife and children.

Chapter 12

ON THE LAND

The tailors' shop work was the least disagreeable that I had had to do during my imprisonment. I did it as best as my technical ignorance would permit, but I was now neither fit nor quick enough, to satisfy the ever-increasing demands of the norm maniacs. My paralysis partially returned at one point. The authorities rejected me, and I was sent to work on the land.

This might have been unpleasant but, for two reasons, I did not regret the change. I had a lifelong love of the country, and I shall never forget the beauty of the Russian landscape.

We would start out at dawn when a silvery mist still hung over the trees. The sky gradually turned yellow and little breezes carried with them the smell of hay. Then one would catch the first faint voices of the forest, which was full of wild life. Several times I found traces of bears and we frequently came upon elk, wolves and wild boar, not to mention the smaller animals and birds. There were eagles, ravens, capercaillie and black-cock, which the Russian prisoners somehow managed to trap. I recall observing shafts of silver light above the marshes and the movement of wild geese high overhead, and longing for my shot-gun.

I often discussed the richness of the wild life and the opportunities for sport with a German in our brigade, Dr. Walter Schmidt later a West German diplomat. We agreed that this was one of the most beautiful countries in the world.

"I bet you that one day," he laughed, "the present system will be swept away and we shall be able to come back with our shot-guns and our fishing rods."

The rivers teemed with fish. During the mid-day break, we would try catching them in the baskets we used for our work. Some of the Russians would fashion traps out of the reeds and others could even catch the fish in their bare hands, eating them raw with salt. Once, we saw a battle between an otter and a giant pike amidst such splashing that we thought someone must have fallen into the river.

Apart from these distractions I was fascinated, while working on the land, to see the collective farm system in action. I had some theoretical knowledge of them from the propaganda films which had been shown in the dining hall every month. In one, I had seen the collective which the wife and son of President Roosevelt had been shown. Their remarks indicated that the Americans were favourably impressed.

There were many well-organised collective farms in Russia, especially near the railway lines, but they were only a fraction of the great collective system which extended throughout the Soviet Union. Russian agriculture experts who were our fellow prisoners were much amused by these films. "We Russians have always known how to cheat the world," they said. "When will the world wake up to reality? If it was a Potemkin (1) Russia in the time of Catherine the Great, it is even more a Potemkin Russia

---

1. Grigory Aleksandrovich Potemkin, (1739-1791) a favourite of Catherine II, had concealed the weak points of the régime, and is celebrated chiefly for his "Potemkin villages" which were specially built to impress foreigners with the prosperity of rural Russia. They were built for the occasion, in cheap but showy materials which lasted only a short time.

today. Only on a greater scale. Those distinguished American visitors are unaware that our livestock was reduced by this collective system to ten per cent of what it was in 1914".

The Russians were right. Foreigners who visited these farms had not the slightest idea of what was happening in Russian agriculture. They went to show-places full of beautiful smiling maidens in national costume, model housing estates, farm hospitals, new communal cinemas and cultural amenities. If they were to dig deeper, they would have been most surprised at the contrast between the real collectives and these differed entities.

The State which entities dealt scientifically with husbandry and agricultural improvements, and with the production of quality crops, were relatively well run. They were similar to most European farms. But they were experimental farms, and there are few of them. The ordinary collectives which produced food for the nation, not only from agriculture, but by stock breeding, fishing and even hunting, are quite different.

My Russian and Ukrainian farming friends told me that the collective I worked in was worth close examination as it was typical and repeated over millions of square kilometres. Each collective then consisted of some six hundred hectares, even though later, through amalgamation, they were increased between five and twenty fold, and were worked by three hundred and fifty peasants. This was ten times as many as were necessary, or could be supported by the land. Ours had three cows and thirty goats, all of them small, lean and neglected. The horses were not much better, spavined and broken-backed, with disproportionately large heads; they looked in need of crutches. The work was almost exclusively manual, even the harrow being drawn by men or women, because there were no tractors, and the horses were unfit. Humans ploughed, hoed, sowed, dug; about fifty working in a line with their spades. Most were women or children, or men over sixty, as the younger ones were needed in the factores.

Although tractor stations had been installed throughout the province, the machines were needed elsewhere, or were out of order, for we never saw them. The few which we were lent were almost unusable, because no one knew how to maintain them. Their lubricating oil had been stolen by the peasants and sold on the black market.

It was the same with livestock. The cows and horses were starving, because the fodder had been eaten by the peasants. They also stole, or ate, the seeds they were supposed to sow. In the spring, they prepared the soil for sowing, but when autumn and harvest-time arrived, and everyone expected a crop, nothing appeared. If a culprit was discovered, he would be given ten years for "sabotage." But this did not make "a blade grow where no blade was."

Living conditions for the peasants were correspondingly wretched. The cottages, or hovels, were dirty and smelly, overrun with mobs of bare-footed, half-naked children in rags, who had never ever drunk cows milk. They might occasionally have had a little goats' milk; but few peasants could afford a goat. Child mortality was devastating; but if so many infants had not died, the country would have been overpopulated. Nearly all the women were pregnant in the spring, like their cows.

These peasants belonged to the Mordvin nation of

forest dwellers, a forgotten, struggling little community. They had been reduced by forced migration to a fraction of their original size, but were trying to preserve their nationality and traditions as best as they could. Their children often came to the camp, or to our working parties, with water, asking if they might have some bread in return. We could not refuse and, if we had any, gave it to them.

Most Mordvin peasant families possessed merely one pair of shoes and one overcoat. Whoever went out in winter whether it was the father, mother or son, donned them, for they were expensive and scarce. Even the wives of the MVD officials who were living in the neighbourhood wore their husbands' military greatcoats. The peasants wore slippers made from the inner bark of trees. Their feet were first wrapped in rags, then the wooden slippers and finally the rags were wound round the legs and tied with string. A workshop in the camp produced these slippers, boiling the bark first to soften it. They were also worn by some of my fellow-prisoners.

Hoping to obtain premiums, the collectives often took part in production competitions, but the rewards for which they risked their lives were generally illusory. They challenged each other, committing themselves to produce so much grain, tomatoes, or carrots, above the previous year's production. They sent enthusiastic telegrams to Stalin, and the newspaper *Pravda*, and received effusive replies, which they quoted to everybody. But how could they know what their harvest would produce? Everything depended, first on the weather and secondly, on a sound economy. The first was God-given; the second was non-existant.

This form of "Socialist" competition was universal

throughout the U.S.S.R., not only for groups but also for individuals, the *Stakhanovites* or new Soviet heroes. The *Stakhanovites* were the men or women who surpassed the limits of human endeavour in any given field of production, agricultural or industrial. Exceptional *Stakhanovites* were sent to meet the great 'Red Tsar' Stalin in Moscow, for handshakes and back-slapping.

The glamour and glory which surrounded these heroes seldom lasted. Sooner or later, the human machine failed to maintain such high standards, and broke down. The laws of nature would not allow the misuse of the human body. In a year or two the *Stakhanovites* had become forgotten men, sometimes even, in their desire to achieve the exaggerated norm, "saboteurs."

These competitions also took place in our prison camps, although we were not allowed to use the sacred word, "*Stakhanovites*." Our work maniacs were known as "recordists."

Chapter 13

THE "SAINTS"

People have often asked me what enabled prisoners to remain sane and survive in these concentration camps. Naturally, physique was of importance. The infirm and the old stood little chance of resisting the intense cold and the excessive work. Apart from this, education was a great advantage for it supplied mental resources. Men like Csomos and Bruzhas were helped by their sense of humour. But above all, as I myself discovered it, was faith which kept people human.

Outstanding in the camps were the priests of the various denominations. The other prisoners will always remember how much they did. Their wisdom and philosophical calm in the midst of so much unhappiness and suffering gave us the necessary courage and spirtual force to continue. They set aside their own tragedies, such as the memories of the families which they, too, had left behind, to help the rest of us. They somehow organised prayers, services, and occasionally choir singing, and constantly diverted our minds. I remember particularly my first confession in prision. It was to an old Ukrainian Uniat priest in the corner of an overcrowded cell in Lvov. He gave me absolution and told me to put my faith and trust in God, because only thus would I have the moral courage to face the future.

The most distinguished of the priests I met was Slipei, the Metropolitan Archbishop of Lvov, head of the Uniat church which observes Greek Rites but recognises the Pope; its adherants are mostly Ukrainians, but it also embraces Rumanians and Hungarians. The arrival of this bishop gave us fresh hope at a time when we were much in need of consolation. A man of his moral stature was able to provide it. He was no longer young, having spent many years in Russian captivity. The official Russian Church authorities, the new Orthodox Church recreated by Stalin, had done their best to persuade him to join them but found him unyielding. However, they had approached his subordinates and had, in some cases, been successful.

The Achilles' heel of most of these Uniat priests was their families. Only to support their wives and children did some of them yield, knowing that they would otherwise be sent to prison and their families would starve. The majority refused to deny their faith, thereby suffering the same fate as their leader. But those who yielded to Communist demands were later to receive their reward at the hands of the people. The partisan movement, headed by the Ukrainians, was merciless to apostates. Many renegade priests were assassinated.

The Roman Catholic priests were luckier than the Uniats because they were unmarried and could not be blackmailed through their families. One of these, a Hungarian Benedictine, Tibor Meszaros, who had been master of ceremonies to Cardinal Mindszenty in Hungary, used to say Mass daily, and prisoners from all over the camp would attend; we would also make our confessions to him. Even the bandits respected him. If they happened to be in the room, they would sit quietly and not disturb the service. Sometimes, they even undertook to stand guard at the door, and warn us when authorities were approaching.

Religious services were strictly forbidden; even to

say one's prayers was regarded as a demonstration against the Communist system. The services were therefore clandestine. The Catholic priests would often say Mass at night, in their own bunks, lying or half-kneeling. (1)

Another Catholic priest who made a great impression on us was an Italian Jesuit, Father Leoni. He had been sent by the Holy See to Odessa towards the end of the war, when Russia and the West were allied. When the alliance split, he was arrested as a spy and sentenced to twenty-five years' imprisonment. He had been with us for ten years, and had somehow always managed to give religious instruction and even perform missionary work. His gently smiling face concealed great strength of character, and gave us immense support. On one occasion he revealed his courage in an unforgettable way.

The authorities had impertinently introduced the "Dove of Peace", campaign into the camp. Not only did the Soviet Government force their own hundred and eighty million citizens to sign their "Peace Movement" manifesto; but they also required the signatures of their prisoners.

In a corner of our dining barracks, a large stage had been erected with a table on which lay the manifesto. Behind it stood the camp commandant, ten MVD officials and other members of the administrative staff. We prisoners were marched in. The commandant then made a speech in which he said that the Soviet Union had introduced many improvements for the prisoners during the last few years. He wanted us to show our loyalty and gratitude by signing the book on the table before him.

1. It was a very moving moment for me when, in London in 1959, I met Father Tibor Meszaros again and he asked me if I would take orders. He is now in Hungary.

We would thus help the Soviet Union to achieve world peace. He asked us to step forward individually and sign.

As the first prisoner was about to step forward, a loud voice at the back shouted in perfect Russian: "Anyone who puts his name in that book, signs his own death warrant."

For a moment there was silence. "Who said that?" shouted the commandant. We all knew it was Father Leoni. Not a work was uttered. The camp guards ran up and down at the rear in a fruitless seach. Suddenly some of the prisoners began laughing; the laughter turned to cheering, and soon we had all left the barrack room. The officials alone remained, with their empty "Peace" book. Father Leoni was never caught or punished for his outburst which took place after 1953, in the more humane Khrushchev era.

Equally courageous were the Protestant ministers. There were also priests of religions previously unknown to me such as the Armenian Independent Free Catholic Church, which had flourished in the Caucasus. This denomination did not recognise the Pope, but its leaders were Christian in a real sense.

I have spoken of the Mohammedans, who found great solace in their religion. They practised it more openly than other groups, always performing their ritual ablutions. They had a muezzin, a member of the lower order of clergy, who undertook his work among them with self-effacing conscientiousness. Nothing could prevent them from obeying his calls to prayer.

The Buddhists were represented by two shepherds, mystics who were constantly praying, and going about their religious duties in a calm and dignified way. We did not know their language, and they had difficulty in expressing their needs. Other denominations included Nazarenes, Baptists, and various sects which had seceded from the Orthodox Church. They all held most of their services secretly in the evening, or early in the morning, behind the barracks, so as to give the impression of carrying on ordinary conversation.

There was one man whose special religion prescribed three days of religious holiday every week. On these days he would not touch tools, or do work of any kind. In spite of every threat, including a spell in the *karker*, he would not yield. Finally, he was sent to a mental asylum. To the Communists, he was a lunatic.

Another group whom the Communists probably considered as lunatics were the Russian Quakers. Single-minded and dauntless, they had written to Stalin asking him to "return to God and mend his ways," adding that they would forgive him if he did so. This letter must have so surprised the Kremlin authorities that they did nothing about it for several months, warily waiting to see if it was perhaps connected with an assassination plot. When they realised that the Quakers were perfectly sincere in the sentiments they had expressed, they arrested the lot and hurried them off to our camp.

One night towards the end of my imprisonment stands out in my mind. A number of our friends had just left to be repatriated, and a common bond seemed to unite the members of all religions. Not only Catholics and Protestants, but Buddhists and Jews, Orthodox and Jehovah's Witnesses, Baptists and Armenian Independent Free Catholics, all sang the Te Deum together. Although we ourselves were not going home, we rejoiced for our more fortunate friends. An old Greek Orthodox priest said a prayer aloud, and a Protestant minister assisted him. Not even the guards disturbed us that night, even though they could have done so, for we made no secret of the service. One of them even said, "Pray on! It seems there is still someone above who hears your prayers!" This was an old Communist who had fought in the Lenin period.

I had never previously experienced, nor have I experienced since even in the Free Western world in which I now live, dozens of people, of different faiths and nationalities so united in thanksgiving for the good fortune of others.

Chapter 14

THE CYNICS

There was a very different type of prisoner, whom I shall remember as vividly as the priests, the stool-pigeon. There was never a shortage of these unpleasant beings in the camps. I had some unfortunate experiences in early days when I was still ignorant of camp life, and became a dupe to other Hungarians who apparently wanted to talk about friends at home.

The first of these was a Hungarian Army officer who was most aftable. He continually tried to win my confidence by telling me about his connections with the camp kitchen. Apart from the prospect of food, I was pleased to talk to a new friend, particularly a fellow countryman who had, like me, been in the army, and who appeared to civilised and friendly. Several times, I accepted the extra food. Always, with great subtlety, he then managed to turn the conversation to my connections with the West.

"I know you are not a British spy," he said, "but you have spent much time in the West. It would be interesting to know how people live there. I have been here in prison so much longer than you that I am starved for information about the West".

He asked me what I had done in Austria, the names of my friends and of all the interesting people I had met in Vienna while working at British headquarters. I told him a little, but nothing that could incriminate anyone. I soon became very careful about giving names. The Russians could easily kidnap people from Austria, or from any of the other countries occupied by their armies, and accuse them of being Western agents, simply because they once knew me.

When he saw my reticence, he became impatient. He began interrupting, seeking information about more specific things rather than generalities. Once, when he brought me extra food from the kitchen, I was surprised to see him staring at it hungrily. I offered him some.

"No, it's for you," he said. "Go on! You must eat it all."

I asked what he meant by saying I must eat it all. Surely he, not the camp authorities, had obtained it for me. When I told other friends about this, they were most suspicious. Those whom I implicitly trusted told me that they had not said anything about him to me as he appeared to be my friend. However, they informed me that he was frequently to be seen at night leaving his barrack block on the pretext of going to the latrine, but in fact he was visiting the night duty officer in the camp office. Next time he came with food, I told him that I was not hungry.

Another Hungarian in the same mould claimed to be an army major even though I was to discover later that he had not even been an n.c.o. He professed great patriotism, and became so emotional when referring to Hungary that he brought tears to the eyes of some of the younger Hungarians. They were so moved that they were even induced to give him some of their food. By now I had had more experience and told them to beware of this smooth-tongued man. One day I told him to his face, in front of the younger Hungarians, that I did not trust him. He said nothing and appeared as charming as ever, but I knew he was furious. My suspicions were well founded.

Some days later, I was summoned to the commandant's office, where the political officer asked me severely what I had against this fellow countryman? What was our quarrel? This was extremely unsubtle of him, and I laughed out loud. Who else could have informed him of "our quarrel?"

Later I heard from a Hungarian army doctor that he had discovered certain papers which this man had inadvertantly left behind when working in hospital No. 9. Amongst them was a report on the mental condition and general morale of the hungarian prisoners! The doctor confronted the "major" with the document. Although he generally had a ready answer, he was speechless and could only stammer. He then fell on his knees in front of the doctor, and asked him not to tell the other Hungarians. The doctor replied that if he ever came across him in the free world, he would kill him like a mad dog.

Another "charmer" was a German whose name, Rupner, was so similar to mine that we became involved in a curious incident. A former landowner in Galicia, he would talk so brilliantly, in a sophisticated, worldly manner that some of the younger prisoners were mesmerised.

One of the Poles educated me as to Rupner's past. During the German occupation, he had lived in Lvov where he had made a fortune out of Jews wishing to escape to Hungary and Rumania for, although there were anti-Jewish laws in these countries, there were no extermination camps. Rupner owned a large van and, in return for cash or jewellery, he would convey Jews to the border where friends could assist them across. He told them that he had fitted his van with curtains, so that they should not be detected on the journey. In no circumstances, if they valued their lives, should they open the curtains or look out while being transported. The curtains prevented them seeing where they were going. After circling the neighbourhood for an hour or so, he would take them to the headquarters of the local Gestapo in Lvov, and hand them over. These unfortunate Jews were later forced by the Gestapo to write letters to their friends and relations, saying that they had arrived safely in Hungary or Rumania, and recommending them to take the same course. This was a most lucrative traffic for Rupner.

The German also ingeniously managed, while working for the Gestapo, to serve the underground movement against the Germans! He calculated that, whoever won the war, he could be on the winning side. This had evidently not availed him, for here he was, in prison.

Rupner was finally involved in an escape plot, which almost resulted in his death by the prisoners, rather than at the hands of the camp guards. He planned, with four Poles, to escape in the snow over the barbed wire by a fire ladder. When the night came, the other Poles climbed to the top of the ladder as arranged but Rupner, at the last moment, stayed below. These unfortunate men found themselves suddenly illuminated in the beam of a searchlight from the watch tower. The guards had been waiting for them and immediately opened fire. Two were killed, and the others were badly wounded. Rupner remained unscathed.

After this, the Polish and Ukrainian prisoners in the camp held a secret "military tribunal", accusing Rupner of treason. They then solemnly passed sentence of death on him. What occurred then followed the usual pattern. One night some two weeks later, a man wearing a handkerchief around his face broke into Rupner's hut while he was asleep and stabbed him. He had intended to kill him, but was disturbed by a passing guard. His attack was not fatal. Rupner was taken to hospital with his throat badly gashed. It was here that our two names, Rupner and Rupert, became confused.

In the middle of the night some days later, a camp guard came into my barracks and asked for me. "Rup.. Rupp... Ruppert...?" he said. The camp commandant wanted to see me immediately. I did not like these midnight interrogations, so I woke a friend, an Estonian who spoke Russian, and asked him to accompany me as interpreter. In reality, I desired a witness.

When we reached the office, the commandant was extremely angry; he stated that he had summoned only one man, not two and asked which of us was Rupner. I replied that my name was Rupert, not Rupner.

"But you are not Rupner? How long have you been here?"

"Three years," I replied.

He realised that there had been a mistake and began cursing the guard who had summoned me. We were dismissed.

When we returned to our barracks, we told the Poles and Ukrainians about this event. Two of them immediately ran out in the dark to the commandant's office and were just in time to see Rupner arriving, his neck still bandaged. Through the window they watched him talking with the political officer. The conversation lasted an hour and a half.

The Poles and Ukrainians now determined to make another attempt on Rupner's life when he left hospital.

But Rupner was too wily. Somehow, when he recovered, he managed to get transferred to another camp. We heard that he had been sent to Karaganda in Central Asia, far away, where no one knew him.

A less frequent stool-pigeon was the prisoner, often one of our close friends, who was forced to become an informer in order to protect his family. In such cases we generally tried to help him prepare his report and were often able to feed false information to the camp authorities.

One of the tragedies connected with this, which affected me most closely concerned a Balt friend. He was a likeable but naive young man who suffered from leukaemia. The MVD said that if he did not inform about certain prisoners, including me, he would be transferred from his task in the hospital and put, in the depths of winter, to outdoor work. He consulted us about this was advised to give up his hospital work rather than accept such a shameful proposal.

He returned to the MVD officer and indicated that, because his fellow prisoners already suspected him of having obtained his hospital job by duplicity, he could not accept the conditions. The officer retorted that he would report to his superiors that the stubbornness of the young Balt came from his Latvian anti-Communist education and that they would recommend that his family should, for the sake of security, be deported to Siberia.

We again carefully discussed the matter and finally agreed that, because of his family, he should accept the "informing" role, but that we should help him in composing his reports. When this happened we were careful not to be too factual, and we made him emphasise the difficulties he encountered in questioning us.

Unfortunately Harry Anderson, the one-legged

Latvian who had been so good to me, decided to use this as an opportunity for paying off old scores with certain MVD officers in Latvia, where he had been arrested. We advised him against this. But he persuaded the young Latvian to state in his report how, in the course of investigations in Latvia before his arrest, he had bribed certain MVD officers. He also 'disclosed' how he had sent messages through them to his family and how one of these officers had supplied him with news from outside and with cigarettes while he was being interrogated. All these were strictly forbidden practices.

This was, of course, untrue, but the ruse was successful, much too successful. The MVD authorities took this confession very seriously, claiming that they could not allow such corruption in their ranks. An investigation was held in distant Latvia, and two of the officers implicated in his arrest were executed (1).

This was not the end, however. Nearly a year later, our young Latvian friend was accused of having invented the whole story, and was himself threatened with execution. Harry Anderson now behaved, as he always did, with great courage. He went to the MVD authorities and admitted his responsibility for the whole fabrication, which he had persuaded his young countryman to write into his report.

We had warned Harry against this action and as we had feared, everything was to end badly. He was sent to Siberia, his family was deported and Harry Anderson paid with his life. I was later to meet some Russian soldiers who claimed to have been present at his execution.

1. These men were probably the objects of local jealousy in their own ranks and such denunciations by prisoners were often quite sufficient to condemn them.

Chapter 15

STALIN DIES - March 1953

One morning in March 1953, when I had returned for another short spell in the tailors' shop, I was sitting at the bench counting my bits of cloth. A prisoner came over and said quietly as he passed, "The old brute with the moustache is kicking the bucket."

I did not understand and said "Which old brute?"

"The one with the moustache," he repeated.

As a rule this particular prisoner looked undernourished and miserable, but this morning his face was positively radiant. I was unable to comprehend what he meant. However, when I heard him repeating these words to the other prisoners and saw the beams on their faces, I realised. He was referring to Stalin. He told us that he had overheard an official Moscow announcement about the "illness of our great leader" on the camp centre radio.

Within a few minutes, everybody was rushing up and down from one section of the workshop to the other, spreading the news. "Illness," in Soviet terms, could mean only one thing. Stalin was already dead, or at any rate dying.

No one produced his norm that morning. Even the "recordists" neglected their work. The whole place seemed topsy turvy, the entire factory in commotion, buzzing like a disturbed beehive. Short of an announcement that the British and Americans had landed in Moscow, nothing could have sounded more heartening? People started to sing.

I found it particularly revealing to watch the factory managers and the MVD officials. Some looked pleased, and the faces of one or two revealed a satisfacton similar to ours. Others demonstrated their feelings with embarrassed smiles. Some looked really frightened. That day it was easy to tell who were the faithful servants of the regime.

When we returned to the camp that evening, the non-working prisoners were standing at the entrance, waiting to confirm the news. They presumed that we had not heard it, because there were no loudspeakers in the factories, no music or entertainment of any kind, not even the familiar blasts of propaganda. They told us that all day, apart from a few interruptions for news bulletins, Radio Moscow had broadcast only funeral marches by Beethoven and Chopin.

This radio programme continued for two days. Every hour, funeral marches were interspersed with short bulletins about the illness of the dictator which we now realised, must have been fatal. We longed, hoped and prayed for confirmation of his death. No one living in the West can have the least concept as to how this hope dominated our thoughts and conversation for the next forty-eight hours. When his death was announced, beantific smiles, radiance and joy lit up every face!.

A day of national mourning was proclaimed, and preparations were made for us all to "mourn with the nation." Red flags draped with black were hoisted on all official buildings. We were ordered to behave quietly and soberly. But strange, previously unheard of things began to happen. A drunken guard tottered around the camp and muttered to me, "Not only you, but we are happy."

An MVD officer we particularly disliked, who was also half-drunk, prattled on about how he hoped the prisoners would understand why he had been so severe; he had had to obey the inhuman ruler's orders. "His system" he said, "has been as hard on us as on you." And he told us that many guards and MVD officers lived in a state of permanent insecurity, not knowing on what day or at what hour, they too might find themselves with us as fellow prisoners, not guarding us.

These were pleasing signs. To hear these words from Russian officials filled us with hope; and in the next few weeks discipline was relaxed in an astonishing way. The guards and MVD men became quite friendly, and improvements were introduced in our living and working conditions, as well as in our rations. The constant day and night searchings of the barracks stopped. The punitive brigades were disbanded. The solitary confinement *karker* was demolished. When the order for this last measure was given, the prisoners shouted with joy, and we all helped remove the debris of the building amidst the laughter of the officers and guards.

It was not only Stalin's death which was responsible for these improvements. During the summer of 1952, nine months before, a new government decree had improved our rations and, for the first time, we were paid for our work. The latter was no more than pocket money, it is true, but it enabled us to buy a little extra sugar and margarine when they were available.

The brick kilns which had been run by women prisoners, the work previously being considered too light were now taken over by men. Special camps were opened for the elderly and crippled, and some of the old Russians were sent home. A terrible comment on Soviet society was that often their wives and families refused to accept them back, on the grounds that they were unable to feed them. Many women were released and their camps allocated to the opposite sex and some of the men's camps were to be, we were assured, "recreation camps." Recreation! The very word sounded thrilling.

That this not only concerned the Dubrov camps, but was general throughout Russia, became clear when we heard speeches by Malenkov and Khrushchev, to which we were invited to listen on the camp loudspeakers. Khrushchev spoke openly of the faults in the system, referring to "crimes committed by the Stalinist regime!" He admitted that the Soviet Union was unable to compete in quality, or quantity, with the West. He stated that only shoddy goods were produced in most factories and that yield from the land had fallen annually. He revealed that numbers of cattle had diminished by eight million since 1938 and were lower than under the Tsars! It had been madness to enforce centralisation, that only decentralisation could, in the present state of Soviet society, produce consumer goods, and he admitted that neither food not clothing was delivered promptly. In short, he admitted that the great Communist Party had proved unable to meet the requirements of the Russian people.

Even though we had been earning a little pocket money, there had seldom been much to spend it on because sugar, margarine and other fats available in the canteen were sold only to "recordists." Now, anyone who fulfilled his norm could buy a pound of sugar and some margarine three times a month. I also bought a little dried fruit and some course *mahorka* tobacco.

The brigades were divided into several *razryads*, or

work categories, and the pay varied according to which *razryad* one was assigned. If we produced the norm, those like myself in the tailors' shop could earn twenty-eight roubles a month, with which we could buy almost a kilo of margarine.

A further improvement in the lot of political prisoners was the imposition of the death penalty for murder. Until this time, camp murders had been punished merely by imprisonment. This was no deterrent for the bandits. A document announcing the new punishment was passed round, and we had to read and sign it. The authorities thereby implicitly admitted that they had not previously objected to murder in their camps. Indeed, they had, in my opinion, deliberately encouraged it. Later, capital punishment was also introduced for certain cases of violent robbery.

Such long-standing habits of violence cannot be completely eradicated. Savagery cannot be eliminated overnight in a land like Russia. The bandits simply became more careful as to whom they murdered, and how they murdered them. The bloody brawls, however, which had often ended in death or permanent disablement, diminished. Now brawling, for instance, was punishable by a month's detention in the *karkers* where such cells still remained.

Our immediate reaction to Stalin's death had been simply, "Thank God! We may now at least survive!" It was no longer certain that we would be left to rot in the camps. No one had imagined they would ever leave them alive. Our hope had been that the West might finally learn what was happening in the Soviet world and would stop making concessions, and that a war might break out. Now we hoped for a less violent solution - hopes which seemed confirmed when the newspapers (1) informed us that the detentions of all foreign prisoners were to be reinvestigated. Anyone who considered that he had been unjustly sentenced, or maltreated in prison, might submit his plea in writing. We were told to seal the envelopes and put them in a special box in the commandant's office, from where they would be sent unopened to Moscow. This caused tremendous excitement, and for days many prisoners would talk of nothing else but of how they were going to draw up their statements. Those who could not write consulted the literate.

In June 1953 certain categories of younger prisoners were called before the camp commandant and individually interrogated. They were mostly Germans and Hungarians who had been captured during the last stages of the war, after being press-ganged into Hitler's "werewolves" at the age of fourteen or fifteen, or, in the case of the Hungarians, into the *kopjas* youth detachments. They had been too young for the regular army, and could not, after capture, qualify as prisoners of war, so the Russians had tried them as war criminals. Strictly, in international law, they were partisans, or *maquisards*. The Russians never tired of glorifying the feats of *their* partisans, but partisans or

---

1. Pravda and Isveztia. These papers generally arrived in the camp five days late. Those who wished could go at certain hours to hear the "news" read out. Isveztia containd of lies and naïve propaganda, but by reading between the lines, one coud learn something about word politics. Some of us also managed to listen to the about word politics. Some of us also managed to listen to the B. B. C. and the American Radio in Munich. Prisoners who were electricians were electricians were often ordered to repair the radio sets of the camp officials. There were always one or two of thes under repair and, although it was stricly forbidden, they regularly listened to foreign brosdcast. this had gone on for years.

138

the opposing were considered war criminals. This opprobrious label had now changed, the youths became prisoners of war, and in a month of two were on their way home. In the first weeks of June, three hundred and twenty of them were repatriated. We later heard that they had had to wait several months in the Lvov collecting centre, where their cases were carefully re-investigated. Many failed to reach home before December.

There was something extremely moving about the departure of these boys. Personal feuds and quarrels were forgotten and old antipathies between Germans and Poles, temporarily laid aside. Those of us who remained behind came to the gates to see them off and wish them, irrespective of nationality, God-speed.

The Germans left first, in groups of four. Occasionally turning to wave, they marched away to the accompaniment of our cheers. When the Hungarian turn came, I could barely restrain my tears. By bitter personal experience these youths had learned something of our national destiny and the harsh Hungarian fate. Clutching the little sacks which contained their possessions, they set off for home. They too turned to look back and wave at the Hungarians they had left behind.

The camp guards, as if understanding our feelings, closed the gates slowly, to give us time to watch them for as long as possible. We stood there, trying to follow them with our eyes as they disappeared into the distance. They were like a *fata morgana*, a little group marching away, towards happiness.

Chapter 16

DARK SKYS AGAIN - CAMP FIVE
July 1953

Soon there were rumours that more foreigners would be repatriated and that lists were already in the camp commandant's office. All the elderly and women with children under the age of ten had been released, and we hoped that our turn would be next. Weeks passed and turned into months, and we were still at our factory benches. We worked half-heartedly, unable even to concentrate on earning our small salaries. The camp authorities, too, seemed uncertain about us; we were "dangerous criminals," sentenced to twenty-five years' hard labour, and they clearly did not know whether to regard us as permanent or not.

On the other hand, the relaxation or "thaw" continued for us all. Small curtural groups were encouraged. Sport and recreation, basket-ball and football, were organised. Cinema shows became a regular feature of camp life. Musicians among us were allowed to give concerts. Instead of propaganda films about the *kolkhozes*, *Stakhanovites*, or the great production achievements of Soviet industry, we saw films about nature and science, the landscape of Central Asia, the Taiga, the fauna and flora of different countries in the Soviet Union, hunting pictures and geological expeditions. There were some excellent reels on the Bolshoi and Kirov Ballets, and of the bathing resorts in the Caucasus and on the Black Sea, where old palaces had been converted into People's convalescent homes. We saw new hotels in Sochi and

Sukhum, the "common people" as tourists on well organised bus trips and invigorating sea voyages. However, as one of the better informed Russian prisoners indicated, the happy, carefree tourists we saw in these films were mostly *Stakhanovites*. The ordinary holiday markers were previously party members.

We were also supplied with stage props and permitted to construct theatrical decor in the carpentry shop. In the cultural groups, anyone could lecture on his own subject or describe his former activities. Under the title of "Cultural Lectures," we often had some highly critical economic and political discussions, all unfavourable to the Soviet Union.

Another feature of this waiting period was sex. The prisoners who used to meet women, in hospitals and fields, tended to be the younger and more hot-blooded. Most of us, the older and middle-aged, were too tired after work to have sexual urges. But now, with the removal of the constant thought of death, and the improvement in our diet, natural desires again appeared. Some of the middle-aged prisoners began to call at Camp 10, which now contained women. Friendships, platonic, sentimental and amorous, were formed; love letters were written, exchanges and somehow conveyed from camp to camp. This was a time of fleeting meetings, quick acquaintances and furtive loves... I had a German friend named Dietrich who had been kidnapped with his fiancée. Both were sentenced as "American spies." His fiancée had worked in the Camp 10 kitchen. He had rarely been able to see or even correspond with her, from Camp 14. They were now in daily communication, frequently finding some excuse for meeting.

Then came a curious incident, which I did not

understand until some months later, when I was called to Moscow for interrogation in the Lubianka prison. It was connected, although in a most unusual way, with the improvement in our conditions.

A few months after the first groups of prisoners had been repatriated, a senior MBG intelligence officer from the Dubrov headquarters came to interview me. I was called to the camp commandant's office in the middle of the night and interrogated through a German-speaking interpreter, a woman from the German colony on the Volga. I was questioned closely, and my answers carefully noted.

The questions did not concern me, but an old acquaintance called Rosen, who had worked with me in 1947 at the British Commission in Vienna. Although Palestinian by birth, he had become a British subject, and had served in the British Army during the war. He had been kidnapped in Vienna by the Russians in 1950, and was now serving his sentence somewhere in Russia. The MGB official showed me a series of photographs in sets of three, asking me if I recognised any of the people in them. Why, I do not know, but Rosen was always in the middle. Although I was suspicious on these occasions, there seemed no point in denying anything, and I admitted that I had known him. I wondered if Rosen had disclosed that he knew me.

The MGB man consistently compared my evidence, taken in Baden seven years before, with statements evidently made by Rosen, as if seeking contradictions. As my Baden "evidence" had been a complete fabrication by my inquisitors, this was not difficult.

"You maintain that this evidence is not correct then?" he said.

"Certainly," I replied. "It's a tissue of lies. You can start the whole thing again, if you like. We might then arrive at the truth."

"Why haven't you made an application for a review of your case?"

I replied that after what I had suffered I had little confidence in the new Soviet clemency. I suddenly felt despondent, and while this was being recorded I turned desperately to the female interpreter. "Why are they interrogating me again?" I asked. "What do they want? I wish I were dead."

Softly she replied "You don't want to die now when there's a chance of improving your position. Don't worry! All will be well."

That this jovial, middle-aged Volga German should speak so kindly amazed me. At first I though this was some new trap. But I told the truth about Rosen. I said that he had never been involved in espionage. His job had been a subordinate one, like mine, concerned chiefly with the postal services of the British headquarters in Vienna. I suggested that if they interrogated him again he would confirm this, assuming that he be allowed to tell the truth.

The interrogator appeared very surprised. He said that if I was lying, I would damage not only myself but also the interrogators who were now trying to help me. This was an extraordinary remark from a high MGB official, but I said he need not worry; I was telling the truth. I added sarcastically that his colleagues had been given the truth seven years before but they had ignored it. It had cost me this hell in Russia, not to mention the eight months' solitary conferment in Baden, being questioned about a crime I had not committed.

This was almost, though not quite, the end of this curious incident which was, I later learned, concerned with the trial of Beria and his subordinates. They had almost tortured poor Rosen to death.

At this point, when everything pointed to a continuous improvement in our situation, things took a turn for the worse. Slave traders arrived from the Far East again, evil-looking officials with Mongolian type faces. We knew what they were seeking and were frightened that there had been another change in policy. Or was it simply Russian illogicality, Slavic muddle-headedness?

The slave traders graded all the remaining Russian prisoners, and we could only hope that we, as Europeans, would be omitted from this classification. Some young Rumanian prisoners were then called, and our initial fears seemed justified. For two dreadful days, we lost hope and saw Siberia as our future. But it was a mistake; the Rumanians had been interviewed because they had Slavonic sounding names. They were returned to the barracks. The slave traders were selecting only Russians, the young, strong and healthy; anyone over forty or in poor health was rejected. These unfortunate Russians were sent to a large oil refinery near Omsk, and to two new power plants on the rivers Ob and Yenesei in Siberia.

Unfortunately, as the Balts were considered as Russian, a number of our friends were in this group. A heart-breaking and pathetic leave-taking ensued. It was a personal tragedy for me. It meant a break with the Lithuanian poet, Mishkinis who had become one of my closest comrades and possessed many of the endearing qualities of his fellow-countryman, Antonos Bruzhas.

These were days of sadness for us all. After so many years together, we had forgotten how attached we had become, how much we were a part of each other's lives, how much we trusted each other.

Some five hundred of these young men left camp knowing that they had a long journey ahead for they were accompanied by an armed escort. Whenever a group left for another camp, the authorities of the new camp would send an escort. The escorting guards this time were Easterners, from the most distant parts of Russia. Special railway wagons had arrived, well provisioned with food and fuel for a three week journey. This was understandable. These men were a valuable commodity, prize bulls to be kept in fighting trim.

A few weeks later, while we still waited anxiously, we heard that our camp was to be turned over to women and that we were to be transferred. Only the essential technicians were to remain, thirty-five men, mostly cutters and designers in the tailor's shop. The rest of us were regrouped, loaded into railway wagons, and sent to the new and, we hoped, temporary camp before repatriation.

As we left, we saw the women arrive. Those who had envied the men who stayed behind changed their minds. Most of the women were old and crippled peasants with handkerchiefs round their heads. They were pathetic. What, I wondered, could have been the "crime" of these wretched creatures? They probably knew nothing of politics; they did not even know why they were here. We waved and some of them wearily waved back. This was my last recollection of Camp 14.

A number of friends and acquaintances were delighted to see us in the new Camp, No. 5. Those who had been there for some time and who worked indoors, tried to persuade their brigadiers that we were particularly suited to work with them, efficient, skilled and reliable. Had circumstances been different, one might almost have described these happy greetings, these back-slappings and embracings, as a school reunion.

But unfortunately, these generous attempts to put us on indoor work were unsuccessful. The camp commandant disliked foreigners. He intented that the newcomers should have the worst jobs. We were not allowed in the shop which produced radio cabinets, furniture, chess-sets and similar woodwork, for which some of us were, by now, particularly apt. Although winter had arrived, we were ordered to the brick-yards.

Nowhere else throughout the world do brickyards operate in winter, because the bricks do not set properly, and it is uneconomical. But such was the need for building material in Russia that these brickyards operated all the year round, sometimes in temperatures of forty degress below zero.

Our Hungarian predecessors had been unwittingly responsible for this, not because they had worked badly, but because they had worked well - too well, as the commandant mentioned in his opennig speech: "I hope you will be worthy successors of your departed compatriots." Other prisoners told us that the work of one Hungarian in the brickyard equalled that of four other prisoners. Our fellow countrymen had become norm maniacs.

We had to hew the clay with picks from open-cast mines as hard as rock. We then pushed it in trolleys to an elevator belt which conveyed it to the factories. Hundreds of kilos had to be carted daily, and there were several accidents.

It was unfortunate, too, that the medical services of Camp 5 were in the hands of equally vindictive officials. Some of our friends said that these officials were envious because they suspected that we would eventually go home. The head of the medical staff was a women major, wearing the military uniform, epaulettes and badges of rank of the MVD. She was a stunted cripple and was said to be jealous of anyone with a normal boby. If we fell ill or had an accident at work, we could expect little sympathy. Her principle appeared to be that no one with a temperature below 100 should be admitted to hospitel. We had a number of tubercular prisoners in our group, who lived in a perpetual state of low fever, with a temperature which never quite reached 100 degrees. Their long, half feverish illness continued while they worked in the brickyards, and when the acute stage of the disease set in, it was too late. Some died in hospital shortly after admission.

The only encouraging feature of these months in Camp 5 was that we were told that "the judical committee of the Supreme Soviet has granted correspondence rights to foreigners." In simple langage, this meant that we could write one postcasrd a month to friends and relations. Our families had not heard from us since 1947, and the effect on our morale was tremendous. We were given a Moscow camp number and a personal subnumber. The cards had a blank reply sheet for our correspondents to reply. We were also warned that if we wrote anything objectionable the card would be destroyed, and we would not be notified. I remember how difficult it was after so many years without writing, to fill these cards. It took me three days to compose mine. My hand shook as I wrote.

We now underwent what seemed to be another set-back. A group of Germans, young military prisoners of war who had been released some months before, arrived back in our camp, together with many youths who had been captured during the East Berlin uprising of 17th July, 1953. They had been on their way home and had almost left Russia, when the authorities had changed their minds. They were now being sent to work in Siberia. They were desperate and convinced that, after the Berlin affair, there had been a sudden deterioration in the international situation and that the relaxation period was over. We had noticed, too, that no new lists of foreigners for repatriation were being posted. After nine months of hope and longing, since that great day when Stalin had died, were we soon to find ourselves back where we were?

When things looked black indeed, my fate was to change and my personal salvation come about.

Chapter 17

SUMMONED TO MOSCOW - January 1954

On the evening of the 10th January, 1954, one of the assistants in the *nariarchiks'* office, a Latvian boy to whom I used secretly to teach English, excitedly ran into our hut. He came up to me smiling and told me I was to go to the central store and change into new clothes *without a number*! He stood blinking, I remember now how happy the boy, a prisoner himself was on my behalf. "Isn't it wonderful!" he said. "You're being freed. We've had special instructions to prepare you for a journey. You leave at five to-morrow."

I could hardly believe my ears as friends came up to congratulate me. I did not sleep much that night because they were constantly coming over to my bunk with the names and addresses of relations they wished me to visit, or communicate with, in the West. Everybody, even the Germans, asked me to take messages. It would have been unwise to write down names, so I tried to memorise them. But such was my excitement that, although my memory had greatly improved during imprisonment, I soon forgot evey one of them.

The next morning my friends came to the camp gates to see me off. One of them, an old Ukrainian priest, insisted on giving me his rosary. As I walked away, I looked back on their faces at the gates, happy and smiling, waving until I was out of sight. I felt a lump rise in my throat. They were happy for my sake, but what about their future? The two guards who accompanied me, although armed with machine guns, were also in the best of spirits. One of them kept laughing and repeating, "*Domoy! Domoy!*" (Home! Home!) I was deeply touched that all these people who lived in the camps were prepared to forget their own troubles because of my good fortune.

I was taken first to Camp 18 at Potyma, a large railway junction on the main Moscow-Kuibyshev line. This was a good sign for this camp was a receiving and distributing centre for prisoners in the entire Dubrov area. It had a section for those about to be repatriated. However, on arrival I was placed in the quarantine section among prisoners who where about to start their sentences. By some error, the new arrivals had ben put with those about to be freed, thereby increasing the sadness of the former, and diminishing the joy of the latter.

The following morning, I was called before the camp commandant who told me that I was to be interviewed by "very important people". He recommended that I keep my mouth shut about conditions in the Dubrov camps. "You may have to return here," he said. "And if you don't behave yourself, we shall know how to take care of you when you come back."

I was taken aback by this, and realised from his reference to "very important people," that I was still far from being freed.

I spent three weeks in this camp before being taken one morning, with a small group of prisoners, to Potyma railway station where we were to have boarded a west-bound train. When the train arrived, it had no prisoners' compartments, so we were marched back to camp, to await the same train the following day. This train was so full of prisoners that there was no room for us, so we again had to return. This procedure was repeated on four consecutive days, until finally the authorities, who evidently wanted at all costs to get rid of us, put us on the next train with prisoner compartments, regardless of its destination. They evidently calculated that we *might* find a station somewhere on the way, where there *might* be some empty carriages, and they *might* be going in the right direction. Such were Soviet methods. In this way we travelled east towards the Volga for sixty hours, finally arriving at Kuibyshev. Here we spent several days in the local prison, before being marched to the station and locked into some wagons. Twenty-four hours later, the train began to move. Judging from the position of the sun, we were at last going west.

In spite of this muddle, the method of locking us in the wagons was efficient. The prisoners' carriages were divided into several compartments, each with a grille door leading to the corridor, and there were no windows. The outside of the coach was made of sheet metal, but the interior was of wood, containing benches and four tier bunks. The grilles were fastened with multiple locks, as in ordinary goals. These prison wagons were an important and essential part of Russian rolling-stock, and were used in conjunction with the ordinary goods service. But when the journey was urgent, as in our case, they would be attached to a transcontinental passenger train. In this way, we travelled along next to coaches full of civilian passengers.

We continued like this for three days, the train stopping at rural stations to pick up new groups of prisoners. They were mostly peasants, clerks or accountants from collective farms, who had been arrested for speculation or falsification of accounts. There was also a number of hardened criminals in chains. The various categories of prisoner were carefully segregated in the wagons. The common criminals or *bitovoys* were separated from us; the political prisoners and men and women were in different compartments.

Only four of us came from the Dubrov camps, two elderly Russians, a young Russian soldier and myself. The old Russians were being taken to a nursing home in Moscow, because their peasant families had refused to have them back at home. In the neighbouring compartment were a number of women prisoners, mostly *bitovoys* who had been convicted of common crimes, pickpockets and prostitutes. They spent their time singing coarse songs and provoking the guards. Our compartment was next to the lavatory, and we could observe everyone as they passed. One of these female *bitovoys* on her way provocatively flaunted her breasts from under a camp greatcoat. This caused a great flurry among the younger men.

One evening when she was on her way to the lavatory, she moved close to the door, and allowed the young Russian soldier in our compartment to fondle her through the grille. The amorous sounds they made continued for at least five minutes, waking up the guard who was dozing at the end of the corridor. He started shouting but the *bitovoy* hurdled obscenities, suggesting that, if he was envious, he might take his turn.

Knowing the guards, I was not surprised at his taking advantage of this. Towards dawn the following morning, I woke to see them openly making love in the corridor. I slept near the grille door, and another of the young Russians who was also awake, pleaded with me to change bunks, so that he could have a better view. He became immensely excited and hysterical with lust. Finally, the girl took pity on him. After she had left the guard, she came close to the grille and allowed him a repeat performance through the bars.

After four days, the Russians in our compartment announced that we were approaching Moscow. They had been permitted to look through the bars of the corridor window. On one of my excursions to the lavatory, I also managed to get a glimpse of the barren landscape. A few old wooden huts, cottages and dilapidated collective farms were the only signs of human habitation; not a house, not a man, not even an animal was in sight. We might have been on the moon. As we approached Moscow a few people and houses appeared, but both looked equally forlorn.

We were nearly an hour passing through the suburbs as the train semed to make a detour of the city, finally stopping at a grimy station where we alighted on an empty platform. Here we were immediately surrounded by a posse of Security police, who separated us into groups, and allotted us to black armoured vans. We were put in the front, but through the window of the rear which was occupied by the guards, I had my first glimpse of Moscow. Here at last was the Communist "Holy City", the hub of those millions of idealists and naive people who believed in Communism.

The citizens in the streets stared at our van, which had priority over other vehicles. No doubt they had seen a Black Maria before. As we approached the centre of the city, I noticed that the people looked very different from the "free" Russians outside the camps I had known during my seven years in the country. They were better dressed, in fur hats, heavy overcoats and solid boots. The coarse quilted overalls which were such a feature in the country and the camps were not to be seen here.

The van stopped a number of times, to deposit prisoners at various goals in different parts of the city. The receiving process at each was very slow. The journey took two hours. At last we crossed a bridge and the outlines of the Kremlin loomed ahead. We passed a number of low buildings and I remember seeing two old ladies on the road behind us, one of whom noticed our van and drew it to her friend's attention. The two women stared, and then rapidly turned and walked off without looking back. The arrival of a black van at the tall building ahead evidently meant much to them. I had not perceived that we were arriving at the infamous Lubianka prison.

Chapter 18

THE LUBIANKA - February 1954

The Lubianka's notoriety dates from the earliest days of the Bolshevist revolution when it was the headquarters of the origianal Communist secret police, the Cheka, and later of the OGPU. In 1922 its chief was Dzerzhinsky, who was responsible for the execution of many thousands of "class enemies" within the prison walls.

A Russian Socialist once said that fate had provided for the interests of the Cheka in advance, by establishing a building hermetically sealed by lofty walls in the very heart of Moscow. I was built by a pre-revolutionary insurance company. When it was taken over by the Cheka, they installed cells and fitted out cellars beneath the internal courtyards. Prisoners were executed in the cellars while truck motors were revved to drown the noise of the shots. During the Second World War, large additions were made to turn the Lubianka into a kind of fortress.

From the outside the prison looks like any of the large central Moscow buildings. Nearby are the Science and Education Ministry, theatres and several foreign Embassies. As a result, it presents a harmless, even a friendly appearance from outside. But this impression changes immediately its threshold is crossed.

The identity cards and documents of our driver and guards, as well as of the prisoners, were examined at the gate, and again on entry to the main courtyard. In front of an interior building, whose entrance at the head of an impressive marble staircase consisted of copper-sheeted double doors, I was ordered to get out. My documents were handed over to an MVD officer, who immediately asked me, "Have you been well treated?" and, "Has anything been stolen from you?" I said that I had no complaints, and he escorted me into a small windowless room. He asked if I was hungry, and I told him that I was, as I had eaten only salted herring and black bread on my journey. He smiled and said that I should have a meal immediately.

This officer, a captain, reassured me with his friendly manner, for I was by now a little apprehensive. He went out, and a man in a smart chef's uniform brought me an aluminium bowl of fish soup and something resembling macaroni. Having eaten nothing like this for eight years, I had almost forgotten that such food existed. As I ate, my stomach seemed to glow and expand.

I sat alone in the windowless room for over an hour, determined to be optimistic. All this must surely lead to my release. But memories of the past eight years kept on returning. All the sad and tragic events of my captivity passed before my mind, and I remembered those fleeting moments of happiness with my friends, Antonos Bruzhas, Harry Anderson and Miklos Csomos. They all came flooding back, and they seemed to me already memories of some distant dream world. Had I really lived through it all?

For the last nine months I had looked only forward, shutting out the past, refusing to remember the barbed wire, the working brigades, the palisades, the *karker* and the grey monotony of prison life. I thought, too, of those Hungarian boys returning home, the unforgettable look on their faces as they left; then, less reassuring, of those other Hungarians I had left behing smiling, waving as I too, left. They had believed that I was returning home. But here I was, in the Lubianka prison in Moscow. What was going to be my fate?

I was daydreaming, when an orderly came in and called me to follow him. I accompanied him, in a daze, hardly daring to hope that this would continue, half afraid that something unforeseen would plunge me back into my tortured dream-world.

An officer and two N. C. Os met us outside and took me across the courtyard to a seven-storey building in the centre of the square. This, too, was closely guarded, and all of us, my escorts included, were allowed to enter only after re-examination of our documents. The security precautions inside, along a labyrinth of corridors, were equally elaborate. A number of multi-coloured lights continually flashed. I learnt later that whenever a certain colour appeared, it indicated either that an important MVD officer was passing, or that another prisoner was being conveyed along the corridors. When this happened,
I was made to turn and face the wall. This prison was unlike any other I had seen in Russia, clean, well-swept, eerily silent due to the rubber floors, and staffed by guards in well-cut green uniforms who reminded me of the old German Imperial *Waffenrock*.

We went up several flights of stairs, and I was handed over to a goaler who also smiled in a friendly way, and warned me that I must talk quietly. He whispered, and I suddenly felt, in this sepulchral atmosphere, that I had entered some kind of new twentieth-century Gothic cathedral.

My cell, which was larger than any I had experienced

before, contained a camp bed and a table. High on the wall was a large grille window, most of which was covered by a plank, so that only a patch of sky was visible at the top. The cell was centrally heated by a radiator behind an iron screen.

The goaler asked if I smoked. I told him that my pipe was in my bag, which had been taken at the gates. He indicated that I would be allowed all my personal possessions, and would be provided with a daily tobacco ration. The only time I could be in bed was between retreat at night and reveille in the morning. If I wanted anything, I was to raise my arm when a guard passed my window. If I had complaints, I was to make them.

In spite of this civilised reception, I was still apprehensive. I had hoped that the visit to Moscow would be connected with my release. Perhaps I had been over optimistic. I cursed myself for having asked one of the first young Hungarians to be repatriated some months before, to take a message to some friends in England. Perhaps he had not been released. Perhaps they had cross-examined him and learned of my message?

After three days, the goaler asked me if I would like to read. As Hungarian books were not available, I requested English and German authors. He brought me a curious selection, including a medieval religious romance by E. Wiechert about Heinrich von Plauen, the last Grand Master of the German Catholic Knights. Another dealt with modern aspects of democracy, but from a Communist point of view. I also re-read *Oliver Twist* in English, a bowdlerised version, concentrating largely on the poverty in nineteenth-century England.

I was allowed daily exercise. A special exercise track had been constructed on the seventh floor of my prison block, at the end of which stood two guards armed with machine guns. As I walked, I was aware of the streets of Moscow below; they were not visible, but the noise and hubbub of a great city surged up. This remote proximity to the capital of the nation which had oppressed me for eight years was so dispiriting that I decided to abandon exercising in favour of my solitary cell, with only my books and thoughts. But all kinds of fears, self-created fears no doubt, perpetually possessed me. When a prisoner is perpetually left alone in a cell, even if well treated, his imagination becomes extraordinarily fertile. At one point, I remember becoming distracted because the reply postcard which I had sent my family from Camp 5 had not been returned. I wondered if they had received it, or if I had written something which would involve me in fresh trouble.

I lost count of the days, but weeks must have passed, during which I spoke not a word. Time seemed to have stopped. Only the regular lowering of the hatch when the guard peered in through the grille, or deposited my food, gave event to my life. Worried and tired, unable to concentrate, I even began to lose interest in reading.

One day I was taken to the prison dentist, imagining that my teeth, which were in very poor condition, were going to be repaired. His surgery was well-equipped with modern American appliances. But all he wanted was to make an inventory of my teeth and record the topography of my mouth.

Hallucinations now began to afflict me, accompanied by strange buzzings and hummings in my head. I heard, or thought I heard, high-pitched, then low-pitched, sounds. At night, a curious tinkling music came to me. I wondered if these sounds were perhaps inner voices, the result of some neurosis or derangement of mind, the effect perhaps of my cerebral haemorrhage. Was I going mad? After seven years of prison life, had I lost my reason? I was later told that they could have been produced by the so-called *yagoda* siren, a horn emitting high-pitched notes calculated to grate on the prisoners nerves, invented by Yagoda, one of the first chiefs of the Soviet security police.

At last, after many weary weeks, the door of my cell opened one morning. A new goaler came in and whispered, "*Kak familiya*?", "What's your name?" I said: "Rupert." "*Podyom*!", "Come on!" He led me downstairs to the door and handed me over to two guards who were waiting for me. They took me across the central courtyard, and into a large building with elaborate wrought-iron gates. Here, I found myself in a veritable palace. The wood-panelled corridors were full of Samarkand and Tashkent carpets. Expensive French paintings, furniture and console tables lined the walls. I did not know it at the time, but this turned out to be the "Holy of Holies", the headquarters of the MGB Secret Police.

I was escorted into an office which was equally well furnished, with leather arm-chairs and plush carpets. I was confronted at a desk by a fat Russian Air Force officer who looked like Goering. He wore the official Communist smile and was extremely jovial. He dismissed the guard and offered me a cigarette. "*Kak dyela*!", "How are you?" he said, motioning me to one of the easy-chairs. He spoke Russian, and asked why I had not learnt the language during my stay in his country. I could speak a little, but I told him frankly that apart from not having much inclination, learning foreign languages in the camps had been forbidden.

He smiled. "What a pity you didn't learn our language!"

"I was not allowed to," I repeated

"That was a mistake," he said.

He sent for an interpreter, and said he wanted me to tell him everything about myself, my prison experiences, my state of health, my treatment, my likes and dislikes - in short, whatever I felt about life. He was kindness personified; but his joviality did not reassure me. What did he want? If I was to be pardoned and released, why had I been brought before this man, in this noiseless prison?

The interpreter, a tall immaculately-dressed officer, entered and asked what languages I spoke. I told him that my previous interrogations by Russians in Baden had been in German, but that they had been inaccurately transcribed.

"Rest assured," he replied in excellent German, "all you say will be translated faithfully. It will be read out to you before it is put on record."

I was far from convinced. "Good God!" I thought. "After seven years of prison, here are records, minutes and interrogations again!"

We now moved to a round table and sat in leather arm-chairs, smoking cigarettes. The Russian Air Force officer again made inquiries about conditions in the camps in which I had been. He asked if there were great differences in the treatment of prisoners in each and how they compared with this prison. His civility and jokes about my time in Russia seemed to make a mockery of all I had gone through. It made me suspicious.

He asked me if I needed anything. I replied that I had no money.

"Well, you shall have some," he said. "What make of tobacco do you like?"

"*Mahorka*," I replied automatically.

The two laughed, and suggested that I might appreciate something better.

"No," I said. "I'm used to *mahorka* now. I've been smoking it for years."

Knowing that Soviet promises were broken I was very sceptical, particularly when they retreated into a corner and conversed in whispers. When the interpreter returned, he asked me if I knew why I was here. I said I did not.

"I will explain then," he said. "You are going to be cross-examined as a witness. We need your testimony. You must be very careful to tell the truth, and nothing but the truth. I must warn you that if you commit perjury, you are liable to a further two years' imprisonment. We don't want you to be frightened of talking about anyone, however important he may be. Or whatever his nationality. Russians included. A general, a colonel, anyone. All we want is the truth."

I could not think what this meant. I had heard that several high-ranking officers had been arrested. Hungarians, Germans and French, they had already been tried, and were in prison.

"Who is this important officer?" I asked.

"It is not for you to ask questions," he retorted smiling, "that is our business".

Suddenly I recognised, on the interrogator's desk, the original records of my interrogations in Baden which took place years before. They were neatly bound in a volume. I then began to suspect what this was all about. Some of the pages were marked, and the fat air force officer began turning. He read out various passages, asking how true they were. I told him that they were a pack of lies. I had apparently admitted having organised a spy ring and several secret agents and to have been in Italy for this purpose. I had never visited the country in my life! Having admitted all this, he said, did I not consider that I have deserved my sentence?

"I made no such admissions," I said.

He continued to ask me about my spy activities.

"You have confessed it yourself," he said. "Here"; he tapped the document, and read out further monstrous statements. "You state that this is all untrue then? With a clear conscience?"

"Of course," I said. "With the clearest conscience."

"But how is it possible?" he said, affecting to be surprised. "This is your own personal record. Try to think hard. Try to remember. Perhaps after all these years your memory is not reliable. You may have forgotten what you said.

"I know perfectly well what I said."

He read out further passages where I had apparently mentioned the names of relations and friends in Vienna, as well as members of the British Mission. These had been social and domestic contacts, but my Baden interrogators had interpreted them in their way. They had attempted to incriminate these people because I had known them.

They watched carefully, as each name was read. These men were experts in ininterrogation, and they realised that my astonishment was genuine. "We don't want you to be frightened," the air force officer said at last. "You must realise that you cannot be sentenced for the same crime again. Nothing can make your situation worse. But a lot can make it better." They crossed to the corner and again conferred.

On their return, they put aside the Baden records in favour of another volume. This contained my Statement about Sergeant Rosen taken in Camp 14 in July the year before. They asked about him, and I repeated that he had been no more than a simple postal clerk, whom I had known at the British headquarters in Vienna.

"You can find out everything very easily," I said. "Because Rosen was shanghaied by your Russians. You can compare our statements."

It was now becoming clear how I was to be used as a witness. I realised later that I was playing a part in one of the biggest ever criminal cases, against Beria and his secret police. Accusations against his organisation, due to its brutal methods, had started in 1953, and investigations were still ongoing. Neither Sergeant Rosen, nor me nor any other of the unimportant prisoners whom these men were now interrogating so carefully, would otherwise have been worth all this trouble.

Some two hundred foreign witnesses like myself had been brought to Moscow, solely to help prepare charges. Proof was required concerning the cruelty of Beria's men, the interrogations and tortures of the Stalinist period. What better witnesses could there be than the victims themselves, the false documents claiming to explain their cases and the fictitious minutes? The latter were now causing considerable embarrassment to their authors, as the new Khrushchev regime wanted to find out the truth about the tens of thousands of foreign prisoners on their hands, nearly all accused of espionage. Only a very small proportion were spies. They wanted to rid themselves of the others by repatriating them. The problem was to find out who was who.

Inquiries into Rosen's case continued for days. They also asked me about my relations with Billy Bauer, an Austrian business man, who had several times been my guest at the British officers' club. They appeared quickly satisfied with my replies about him, and rapidly returned to Rosen. My interrogator observed that I was now saying exactly what I had said eight months before, in Camp 14, not what had been recorded in the Baden minutes. They were impressed. Had I not been telling the truth, I could not have repeated my Camp 14 statement verbatim.

"You learnt your lesson well eight months ago," the air force officer said, smiling.

"There was no need to learn it," I said.

"Then you deny the validity of the whole of your original statement? Either we accept your second statement, or we accept the original one. We have to come to a decision on one of them. That is why we intend going into details." They then again asked if there was anything I wanted? I said I was tired of solitary confinement; I would like a cell companion.

The next day I was put into a cell with a young Russian officer. I was suspicious that he might be the familiar stool pigeon, but after two days' conversation, in German, I accepted that he was sincere and I liked him.

He told me he had always been a faithful Communist. He had been a *Komsomol* member in his youth and was educated at the Moscow Military Academy. Later he had been a major on the general staff, and had been wounded in the war. Then he was arrested, for what reason he knew not, and removed from his wife, after three days of marriage. He had already been in prison for four and a half years.

I felt extremely sorry for him. He was very bitter and said that one could never trust one,s friends in Russia, because it was the intrigues of "friends" which had landed him in gaol, on trumped-up charges. But things were better and, as with me, the illegality of his sentence was being investigated. We tried to cheer each other by telling ourselves that each of us would soon be free.

One evening, we listened to jet planes flying over Moscow in preparation for May Day celebrations. It was the first time that I had heard the sound of a jet and he explained that these were the new "reactive" aircraft. I found this news disconcerting. If Soviet industry could make these ghastly things, then the war for which we hoped might not necessarily end in a Western victory. We had been delighted to learn from the Russian newspapers in the camps that the Americans were surrounding the Soviet Union with military bases, and hoped that this would lead to war. The Soviet newspapers identified at least four hundred and twenty of these bases. Every evening between seven and eight p.m. we listened to the bangs and shrieks of these jet planes.

While we were together, an important Government commission, consisting of a general and several officers, came round and talked to us, as usual, in a most amiable manner. The general showed great interest in me, and I sensed that my name was familiar to him. He told me that he was Deputy Chief Public Prosecutor, and that I might tell him anything I wished. I told him I was here as a witness, and that I was guilty of nothing.

"Well, if you consider you are not guilty," he said, "you have presumably appealed for a revision of your case?"

I told him that I had not because I had little confidence in the new régime. This did not appear to annoy him, and he smiled. "Would you like your case to be re-examined - fairly, I mean?", he asked.

I thanked him and said that as I had been here for weeks and they were evidently again going through all my evidence, though clearly in connection with another case, they might as well look into mine. He said that my case was now quite well known.

Shortly after this, my Russian cell companion left and I again found myself alone. It is extraordinary how stimulating companionship is after weeks of solitary confinement. It took me several days to return to my old melancholy. Perhaps, I told myself, they were really re-investigating my case.

When I was next interrogated, I asked the air force officer if they would get it all over and if I were not to be released, to be sent back to the Dubrov camps. I explained that I had been in the camps so long that I liked the company of prisoners. I had begun to feel that prisoners were the only humans with whom I now had a common language; I would probably feel ill at ease with free men.

They laughed, assuring me that this ordeal would not take so long as in the past, and asked me to be patient. I would possibly have to spend two or three weeks more here, but they would do what they could for me.

I went through several more interrogations, always on the same theme, the divergence between my various statements about Sergeant Rosen and his activities in Vienna. The interrogators still tried to confuse and embarrass me by constantly confronting me with the two statements. They occasionally mentioned the possibility of two years' imprisonment for perjury, but in a half-hearted way and laughing as they said it. I was later to learn that the chief interrogator had been very satisfied with my answers, which were used extensively in the charges against Beria's assistants.

Finally they asked about the interrogation methods used in Baden. What kinds of torture or physical punishement had been used? How much time had I spent in solitary confinement? Under what conditions? How had the proceedings of the military tribunal been conducted? With or without a defending counsel? They also wanted to know the exact punishments I had undergone since my arrest. The *karker*. Who were the perpetrators of such atrocities? Did I know their names? I was delighted to tell them all about the AVO headquarters, Andrassy Ut 60 in Budapest, where I had received a beating. At this they looked at each other and shook their heads in horror, or was it mock horror?

"Only the Hungarians were cruel?" asked the interrogator. "What about the Russians in Baden? Who left you for ten months alone in a wet, cold cellar with no exercise? What about their interrogations? And their prison cells, where there was hardly room to stand?"

"Hypocrites," I thought. I still felt that under Stalin, these men had behaved in exactly the same way. Even if they had not tortured people, they had certainly believed in the "let them rot alive in wet and putrid cells" means of interrogation.

"Now we know how our peole behaved in occupied territories," they said piously to each other. "In Vienna, Budapest, Bucharest!" The fat interrogator raised his hands in horror. "Don't I know it! Don't I know it!"

It was an interesting spectacle.

I suddenly felt quite weak and faint. Perhaps these men were not hypocrites. Was it possible, I wondered as I observed them closely, that Stalin's death could really have brought about such change? Perhaps the West and Russia could now meet on common ground. Perhaps a general reconciliation was already in progress. I realised that I was being treated with understanding, almost as an ally. Perhaps I had really achieved something, in helping to condemn Stalinist methods in the occupied territories.

They knew of my conversation with the deputy public prosecutor about the reopening of my case. They asked me where I would go if I was released. They did not appear shocked when I said Great Britain. They seemed well disposed and said that we must all hope for the best; but they refused to commit themselves as regards my future.

The now translated minutes of the questions and answers were brought for me to sign. I read them carefully, found that they were accurate, and willingly signed, at the top and bottom of each page. Here ended a further three months of wearying interrogation which at first I had imagined would be concerned only with my liberty and return to Hungary.

On the 28th April, 1954, over a year after the death of Stalin, I left Lubianka. I still did not know my ultimate destination.

Chapter 19

THE LONG ROAD HOME - May 1954

On an Eastbound prisoners' train, I soon realised that we were back en route to the world of the camps. As I looked through the scratches on the frosted glass in the corridor, I saw that we were returning to a familiar land. I recognised the junction at Potyma; we then turned off south towards Dubrov.

Although completely disillusioned by my visit to Moscow, I looked forward to telling old friends about my abortive time in the great Lubianka and of the interrogators who adopted the new "civilised" approach, while ingeniously using me to their own advantage. "I am a pawn," I said to myself, " and no one cares what happens to pawns. Pawns can quite easily die at work, one cold day in the winter."

I could again see before me the working brigades, less brutal perhaps, but still the same brigades. I could vision the endless early morning *proverkas*, the standing about in Russian snow waiting for something that never happens. Was this really to be my destiny? I, a westerner, who had known civilisation, who was still anxious to achieve something in life - was this the point of it all? Was this why I had been born on this planet?

I was not returned to my old camp. There was an order of which I was unaware, that no prisoner should return to where he had been before. Instead, I was taken to a small camp containing some five hundred prisoners, mostly technicians repairing railway engines and wagons. The less qualified, like myself, were employed at staining railway sleepers with creosote.

It was unhealthy work. Creosote contains a powerful alkali, whose smell in the heat becomes overpowering. It sometimes made me feel quick sick. The automatic stainer affected the skin. Hands and faces became swollen as a result of contact with the creosote, and when water got on the skin, the itch was unbearable. My body was soon a mass of blisters, and my skin black. How unhealthy this work was can be acertained from the fact that we were given half a litre of milk daily, some drunk before, some after work. I had never drunk Russian milk before. I did not know it existed. A prisoner friend, a doctor, told me that milk absorbs alkali and other tar products thus protecting the breathing organs, the glands and the mucous membranes.

Hard as this work was, conditions for the prisoners continued to improve. Our working day was never more than ten hours and the food was much better. We were allowed to write and receive a postcard each month. Red Cros parcels, one of the greatest boons imaginable for a prisoner, began arriving. I shall not forget the generosity of countries like Austria and West Germany who came to the relief, not only of their own people, but of us all. Every day, a hundred and fifty of these parcels arrived (1), each weighing from five to eight kilos and containing food, clothes and medicine.

The food in these parcels was of the highest quality, and very soon all the prisoners were looking better. We even managed to send the Red Cross names of Russian prisoners who were our friends. They too received parcels. If we shared ours with everyone, it meant, on

---

1.   Called *posilka* in Russia, one of the few words of that language I never wish to forget.

average, about one parcel to every ten prisoners, or the equivalent of almost a kilo of extra food per person per day. The parcels also contained a coupon which the addressee filled in as an acknowledgment, and returned to the camp centre. The number of parcels arriving daily finally became so great that auxiliary personnel had to be recruited at the camp post office to deal with them. A further concession was that those who wished to cook the contents of their parcels were allowed to build themselves small kitchens. Whether as a result of the new policy, or of general improvements in Russia, I do not know, but the postal and camp authorities were scrupulously honest with these parcels. There were few complaints of theft or loss.

Another feature of the relaxations was that sport and recreation were now encouraged. One day, I accompanied our football team when they went to play another camp, and to my intense pleasure, Antonos Bruzhas as among the spectators. I told him about my Lubianka experiences and he said, "Of course anything can happen in Russia. But I believe this will lead to your release. And not to Siberia. Where incidentally I want to go now."

"You want to go to *Siberia*!"

He took some photographs from his pocket and showed me his wife, sons and two grandchildren playing with a bear cub. They had been deported to Siberia, but were reasonably contented. He had just heard from them, and had applied to join them there. "Perhaps I can play the organ there, in a Siberian village!"

This is the only case I know of anyone actually wanting to go to Siberia. Much later, I heard that he was granted his wish. Perhaps he is still there.

I also found myself with Miklos Csomos again and the Hungarian politician, Bela Kovacs. Miklos had been sacked from his hospital job for "dishonesty." He had been asked to fill the teeth of certain Russian Secret Police and camp staff with brass; for gold was unobtainable. Unfortunately they supplied him with copper which had oxidised in their mouths, and several had been badly poisoned. For this quite unintentional mistake, he had done a long spell in the *karker*, and here he was, in an ordinary working brigade, irrepressible as ever. "So many Russians the less!", he laughed about the copper teeth.

But these improvements and concessions did not compensate for my unsccessful visit to Moscow. It was now almost a year since the first prisoners had been repatriated and here was I, still in a Russian concentration camp.

An interesting feature of Russian psychology was revealed in the new Khrushchev era. Our camp contained a lot of Russian prisoners, from evey social layer, from the highest intellectuals and army officers down to the poorest *moujiks*. These Russians detested the regime which had imprisoned them; but when Khrushchev, the prototype of the *moujik*, came to power and told them about their grievances in a language comprehensible to everyone, speaking strongly against the past iniquities, the nepotism and injustice of the Stalinist regime, they became mesmerised. Professors, who until now had been the bitterest opponents of the regime, often surpassing us in their hatred of it, could talk of nothing else.

In this new atmosphere, it seemed as if their violent sentiments had swung in an extraordinary *volte-face* to the other extreme, into a burning Slavonic passion. Before, they had talked only of Western help and of the "liberation" they longed for. Now they began to boast of how the Russian nation had at last come into its own. "We have found our soul!" they cried. "Now the West will see what a creative, energetic nation can and will achieve!".

One fanatic said to me: "You Westerners will soon realise the magnificent results which will now derive from the Russian craving for work. You will have to recognise our supremacy. The great eternal Russia is at last resurrected. The vocation for which destiny intended us will at last be accomplished. You, nations and sons of the West, will one day see what our reborn country can do. And Russia will work in the interests of all humanity! In your interest too!"

Here we have the true Russian, governed only by his emotions. In the strange ferment of ideas unloosed by Khrushchev, even the most educated Russians gave themselves away. Their sense of criticism vanished, their instincts revealed them as a half-barbaric people still unacquainted with the reason and logic which had developed in the west.

We must never forget this. Guided by instincts and emotions Russians can do angelic things; but they can also be diabolical. Dostoievsky has put it well. The Russian is an idealist, who is ready to give his life, like a Good Samaritan. Yet he can, a few seconds later, kill the man for whom he would have sacrificed that life. Indeed, sometimes our guards, if not closely supervised, told us to stop working, put down our tools and have a rest, and even shared their bread and tobacco with us.

This was to me, in these last days, one of the most exciting, and yet one of the most disturbing, experiences.

I really began to understand what the words "Russian soul" meant; and I realised that a shrewd and clever leader like Khrushchev, who understood his people, could lead them where he liked. He could certainly use his great power for good; but how sincere was his criticism of the old Stalinist regime? Was it simply the trick of a clever man aware of changing conditions, who knew how to turn mass opinion to his own advantage? Europe's classical history is full of demagogues, Cleon and Hyperbolus in ancient Athens, Cola di Dienzi later in Rome, down to Mussolini and Hitler in our own times, all of whom knew how to mesmerise and exploit the masses.

We Europeans did not know what to think about Khrushchev; we only knew that his coming to power had brought us relief, and for this we were heartily grateful. All concentration camp prisoners, if they were to survive, had to be optimists. We wanted to believe in Khrushchev, to see a splendid portent in him. We no longer thought in terms of a general war, which would gain us our freedom, but of a reconciliation between East and West. We hoped Khrushchev's era had inaugurated a better, happier future for all.

Another sign of changing conditions was the "education" introduced in the form of lectures. Political officers gave them, and they still contained a great deal of propaganda. These men still wanted to impress us with Soviet statistics and no one, save the lecturers themselves, could have believed some of the nonsense they spoke. A lecture which made us laugh was about the poor workers in capitalist countries. In England, America and France, we were told, workers had to queue for bread; Western workers went about in ragged clothes; they were exploited; their governments were helpless when confronted with accidents, epidemics and disease. The lack of medicine was shameful, in the West!

All this, we thought, was one of the many typically bureaucratic muddles. They had somehow got hold of material dating from the Stalin era. When they said that the Soviet Union was far more advanced in these matters even those prisioners who came from the various republics of the Soviet Union, and had never seen the West, were flabbergasted. They said it was inconceivable that anyone could still talk such rubbish.

"These lecturers are either swine or complete imbeciles," a Russian prisoner said to me, adding sadly: "If they go on being so stupid, can one ever hope things will improve?"

We told him to shrug it off as a peculiarity, inseparable from a totalitarian regime, to be treated as an amiable and picturesque eccentricity.

Eventually we realised that we were to be repatriated, although we Hungarians were low on the list. Japanese, Turks, Iranians and French were all before us. It was not until November 1955, two and a half years after the death of Stalin, that our turn came. We were called individually to the camp office, where we had to sign a declaration of release.

Hungarians were divided into two groups. The first granted a *total* amnesty which meant that, in the eyes of the Soviet Union, they were now free men, a tacit admission of their wrongful imprisonment. The second group, to which I belonged, was being repatriated through "an act of clemency." The Soviet Union still considered us "guilty of crimes against the State." This distinction was to have unpleasant consequences for me when I returned to Hungary.

One morning in November our group, accompanied by only two Russian officers and two N. C. Os were marched to the train which was to return us to Hungary. Those who could walk, walked; the old and sick were carried on stretchers, or in horse-drawn carts. To the strains of the Hungarian national anthem, we left the world of concentration camps. Amongst us were Miklos Csomos and Bela Kovacs.

It was a slow train and we stopped at almost every station, but we were allowed to get out and walk about the platforms freely. Before leaving, we had received new unnumbered clothes, and underwear; but to obtain money to buy tobacco, some of the prisoners sold them to the civilian and railway personnel on the platforms. They then re-dressed in their prison clothes.

Despite our wretched condition, there was a jovial atmosphere. We talked and laughed, almost like a group of schoolboys going homo for the holidays. Two of the women, who had been prostitutes in Budapest, "celebrated" by offering themselves *gratis* to anyone who felt inclined!

On reaching Moscow, the Russian officer in charge of us said that the train would wait for twenty-four hours. if we wished to visit the city, we should be back an hour before the train departed. I took advantage of this extraordinary freedom to see the city I had, until now, known only from a prison van.

Half dazed, we wandered the streets, staring in at shop windows most of us had not seen for ten years, contemplating how wonderful it would be to go in and buy. Muscovites were mystified by our strange appearance and clothes, and asked us who we were. When they heard, the good and charitable side of Russian character was displayed. They were deeply emotional, some thrusting money on us, and insisting on taking us to cafés, offering us food and drink. Queues had formed outside the food shops, and when those waiting learned who we were, they insisted on sending us to the front. They tried to reassure us, saying that the hideous experiences we had known would never be repeated. "Papa Khrushchev will be much better," one of them said. "Have no fear! The future is bright. For you, as well as for us."

It was a very moving experience.

We also visited the huge university building where I was delighted to meet, by chance, a number of Hungarian students who were in Moscow on scholarships.
They, too, were moved to tears when they heard wo we were, and threw themselves into our arms. Several said that they were not happy in Moscow, and would like to join us on our journey home. However, to refuse a Moscow scholarshsip was still, in Hungary, almost treason. They took us to see the Kremlin, that building which housed those responsible for so much of our misery; some of us travelled on the Moscow Underground. Other Hungarians seized the occasion, and Muscovite hospitality to get gloriously drunk. Others sought women. Three got lost and missed the train.

We were all late in returning to the station, where we found our escort commander in despair. "Where have you been?" he cried. We've had to hold up the train for you. Come on! In you get!" We could not wait for the three who had failed to arrive, and gave them up for lost. But they were sent on by express, and rejoined us at a country station. The Russian officer in charge was delighted. "Thank God!" he cried again. "How pleased I am to see you! Come and have a drink in the station restaurant! We are as happy as you are that you are all going home!" We all went in. He paid for our drinks.

The train now continued on through the famous forest of Briansk, past Gomel, Lvov, and over the Carpathians. At the Uzsok Pass we crossed the historic, thousand-year-old, Hungarian border, which was no longer our frontier, for Soviet Russia had seized this part in 1945. The train stopped for some minutes here, and we sang the old Hungarian national anthem, and the songs from Kurucz times which recall the greatness of our nation.

We reached Munkacs, another Hungarian town now in Russia, after midnight, but the population had learnt of our arrival. They broke through the police cordon and showered us with their hard-saved little reserves of fruit and food; they embraced us, saying that however much we had suffered, we were at least going home to Hungary; while they had to remain here, under Russian rule. And all this quite openly.

We continued, and at last arrived at Zahony, the new frontier station, where we remained some hours, waiting for a Hungarian train to take us, we hoped, to Budapest. But here, on the border of our own country, one of the worst shocks awaited us.

Chapter 20

A PRISONER IN MY OWN COUNTRY
November 1955

When our train arrived that morning, the Hungarian security police, the AVO, treated us with open hostility. As soon as the Russian officer had handed us over, they loaded us on to prison wagons, which were no more than closed cattle trucks. Armed personnel guarded the platforms. We rolled on, prisoners again, but this time in our own country. Although Russia had sentenced and imprisoned us we had, on this last journey from Dubrov, been treated well by the MVD. Until now we had travelled as though we were free, some of us in Pullman cars. Our own country now received us as criminals.

We continued on for an hour and a half. At Nyiregyháza, the doors were opened and a dense cordon of AVO men, armed with machine guns, closed in on us. They hustled us out, and drove us like sheep into what had once been the barracks of the 4th Hussars where, many years previously, I had spent some weeks as a reserve officer. Now it was an AVO prision.

Of the eight hundred prisoners in this barracks, some two hundred and fifty of us were in the category of those who, like myself, had been released only as an act of Clemency; the Soviets still considered us guilty. As I predicted, we now began to receive very different treatment.

A number of senior AVO officers appeared from Budapest to separate the sheep from the goats, Csomos and I being among the latter. I told the oficer who interrogated me that I had spent almost nine years in Russian concentration camps for crimes I had not committed. But he claimed to know all about me, and replied to my questions regarding the future with coarse and sarcastic threats. The weeding-out process continued for several days, until those of us who had not received the full amnesty had been pin-pointed. The others were given identification papers and released. We were again loaded onto a prison train.

Slowly, too slowly, we advanced across the great Hungarian plain, passing Debrecen, recognised excitedly by those of my fellow prisoners who lived there. When we arrived at Jászbereny, shouting and cursing AVO men again took command, herding us into an old Carmelite Convent, which was now a prison. However, the convent's religious past could not be entirely obliterated. The few remains of frescoes, broken statues and marble angels on the floor, proclaimed it as having been a House of God.

We remained here for several months. It was not until February 1956 that the final phase of my prison life commenced. Bela Kovacs, the former Smallholder minister who was released after a month on account of his poor health, and I were taken to Budapest for further interrogation. I had no idea that this was to be the last, for I now saw life as one vast, endless interrogation.

The AVO officer who questioned me in the Fö Utca in Budapest was, I admit, friendly. He said that he admired my conduct during the war and regretted what had since happened. He only hoped that I would now be prepared to serve the cause of democracy and humanity. Several times he repeated that Hungary needed men like me. Our talents could be well employed in building Socialism! What were my present political views?

I said I had not changed; I was the same man I had been before imprisonment. It was useless to expect me to support communism, after what I had been through. Materialist philosophy was alien to me. My faith was deeply and unshakably Christian, and I would rather die than betray it. Other AVO officers in the room who overheard these words laughed. "There's nothing to be done with him," he said. "He's incurable."

Perhaps because I had spoken of my Christian faith, or perhaps because I had admitted that my sympathies lay with the West, and I intended to go there, I was not released. I was transferred to the national prison near the Rakoskeresztur in Budapest. Here, I found a number of other "Russian prisoners", as the returned Hungarian prisoners were called, who had also not received the full amnesty. Similar attempts had been made to coerce them into collaboration. At one point we told the AVO authorities that we would prefer to return to the camps in Russia. We said we wished to register a complaint to the Russians about their allies, the Hungarians, and their barbaric treatment of prisoners!

While I was here, I fell ill and spent the rest of my captivity in the prison hospital being treated for a variety of minor but irritating afflictions, such as ear trouble, an abcess in the nose and inflammation of the mucous membranes which was probably caused by my recent creosoting work.

Among the other patients in the prison hospital was Gabor Peter, the notorious ex-head of the AVO, who had been arrested some months before and imprisoned for his Beria-like methods. His assistant, Istvan Timar, my old law colleague at university who had been so cruel to me when I was arrested in Budapest in 1947, was also there. It was strange to look up from the yard where I was taking exercise and see Timar at a window, smiling and waving in a friendly way. As I passed, he leant down and said how pleased he was to see me back in Hungary. I shook my fist. The other prisoners, mostly old and sick, sitting by the wall, saw this and rocked with laughter.

One of the patients in my hospital's female ward was the British journalist, Edith Bone, who has since written an account of the terror and inhuman conditions in Rakosi's Hungary. She had come to my country as a *Daily Worker* correspondent several years before. When about to return to England, she was arrested on the usual espionage charge. In those days, under Rakosi, this was simply another way of saying, "You're an Anglo-Saxon". She spent years in a single cell. We did not then know who this dignified old lady was, but whenever we saw her we waved; she gracefully acknowledged our greeting.

The first good news here was the fall of Rakosi in summer, 1956. We felt it could not be long now before we were freed and, in fact, one of the immediate consequences of his fall was to be my release in mid-October, 1956.

Before they dismissed me however, the AVO officers cross-questioned me and told me that they had not forgotten that when I was arrested, I had knocked down one of their officials; I was still relatively strong and active and might offer further resistance to the regime.

They asked me where I would go if I were released. I told them that my chances of beginning a new life seemed to be best in Austria, where I had relations, or in England. They then asked if I really thought I could earn a living abroad, and advised me to stay in Hungary. They went on to speak favourably of my war record, and I believe that it was this that eventually led to my release.

Chapter 21

I GAIN MY FREEDOM & LOSE MY FAMILY
October 1956

The Budapest that greeted me was very different from the city I had known nine years ago. Not only did the people look different, but their attitude and manner had changed. A decade of Communism had altered them beyond recognition. I was a stranger in my own land.

As I walked towards the Western station to take the train to Vacz, where my family were living, people stared at me, but with none of the sympathy I had experienced in Moscow. An elderly porter who knew my father, and had heard of my misfortunes, was the only man in whose eyes I saw understanding. He even tried to give me money. He insisted on taking me to the buffet, where he brought me a glass of wine. His eyes filled with tears, he put his arms around me, and would not let me go.

The man in the ticket office looked at me less sympathetically when I asked for a third-class ticket. There was no such thing in the People's Democracy; I must have been away a very long time! There was only a "wooden bench" class. In the train, I talked to workers on their way home. When they heard where I had been, they became sympathetic but they were also very careful what they said. I understood what it meant to live in Rakosi's Hungary.

The streets of the little town where my family lived were dark and deserted, and when I finally found the house, my reception was as feared. I rapidly became aware of mixed feelings. My wife was glad to see me, but she was also frightened. She had all but given up hope of seeing me again, and did not know if I have been offically released. Perhaps I had escaped! My daughters had been babies when I had left; they looked at me as a stranger. Only their natural good manners were responsible for their affection and joy at seeing their father again. That night, we talked and endlessly discussed the future. There was little sleep in the one room where the family lived.

When I suggested emigrating, if we could obtain a passport, my wife indicated that she still did not wish to leave "the tombs of her ancestors." The few days I spent with my family left me in a haze, uncertain what to do. My eyes, as well as my mind, could not get used to the new environment, to the fact that I no longer lived within four prison walls, that I could exit and enter when I liked. I walked the streets and talked to the people. Everyone was friendly, but they treated me with caution. I felt that all of them, my family included, were still frightened of what I might do or say. A doctor friend told me to get out into the fields, in the open air, to accustom my eyes to space and distance. I went for long walks in the neighbouring hills and sat in the meadows. I tried to adapt myself to freedom.

My old law colleagues told me that they were now organised in lawyers' co-operatives, and that, in the new social and economic conditions of Hungary, there was little point in my trying to take up the work again, as I had no knowledge of socialist law.

After some days I became restless and decided to visit my aged father who lived in the southern part of the country, at Szentes. As my family did not wish to come abroad, I felt that after seeing him, I ought to return, and go into a factory, with a simple, perhaps manual job, which would at least not make me a burden to them.

In the second half of that fateful October 1956, two days before the outbreak of the revolution, of which we suspected nothing, I set out for the south. I had planned to ask a friend to inform my father that I had returned, so that the shock of seeing me again would not be too great. When I arrived, I was so eager to see him that I went straight into his room; we simply stood and stared. We then fell into each other's arms.

He had greatly aged, but he still possessed the inflexible will I had always admired and which had made him oppose both the dictatorships imposed on Hungary between 1920 and 1948. He had never wavered in those dangerous times; nor did he waver to-day. If he had changed physically, mentally he was as alert as ever. We spent two unforgettable days, talking, making plans for my future, neither of us having any inkling of what lay ahead.

The 23rd October, 1956, was the greatest day in Hungarian history since the time of Kossuth. I took no part in the revolution. This was partly because of my physical condition and partly because I did not understand the immediate Hungarian past from which it resulted, such as the revolt of the writers, the dismissal of Rakosi, the rehabilitation of Rajk, Gerö's speech and Titoism. I only saw with my own eyes that Hungarian democracy had begun to stir again in those short halcyon days.

The municipal Government in Szentes was reorganised. It required no directives from the centre, no foreign agents, no hidden underground movement as the Communists later claimed, to create a popular rising.

There was no violence, nor any need for it. Everything was spontaneous; everywhere the most reliable, sober and honest citizens took over the local government, and organised the collection and despatch of food to Budapest. Isolated from the rest of the country, whose railway and postal services were paralysed, they wholeheartedly supported the ideals of the revolution. The various classes, workers, intellectuals, peasants and municipal officials collaborated well in my father's town.

Towards the end of the first successful phase of the revolution, I became worried about my family and felt that I must return. After five or six days, thumbing trucks, I reached Pecs where I went to the house of Bela Kovacs. I had not seen him since we were both in the Jászbereny prison. Most anxious to consult him, I was informed that he had been appointed Minister of Agriculture in the new revolutionary Government. Workers and students had come for him and he had left in such a hurry that he had not even had time to say good-bye to his family.

Still in my old prison clothes, for I had no money to buy civilian ones, and no one had any to give, I went on to Budapest, again obtaining lifts from trucks conveying food to the capital.

On arrival in Budapest on the lst November during the height of the revolution, I immediately went to the headquarters of my old party, the Smallholders, which had been resurrected. Here, I found many old friends who enthusiastically welcomed me and asked me to help in reorganising the party. I said that I was in no condition to do so yet, but that I would be pleased to as soon as my health allowed, and I had arranged my family affairs.

Amongst the friends here was Miklos Csomos who had been sheltering the politician Bela Kovacs during the revolution. As can be imagined, Miklos was busy organising resistance groups and when he heard that I was in Budapest, he telephoned me. It was wonderful to hear his cheerful voice.

"Here we are up to our necks in trouble again!" he chuckled. "We can't escape it. But if you get a chance to go West, take it. You're too ill to do much here. But I'm now completely recovered and I've been eating like a hog. I've just got Uncle Bela out of the Parliament building."

It appeared that he had organised a small group to rescue Bela Kovacs to prevent him falling again into the hands of the Russians. He was also organising groups to relieve the fighters in the Killian Barracks. Much later, after the revolution had collapsed, Miklos managed to escape to Switzerland where he practised as a dentist in Basel. We continued to keep in touch.

Then came the early hours of 4th November, when the Russian tanks invaded Budapest, and we heard Imre Nagy's radio appeal to the country and to the West. He spoke with calm and dignity, and we listened, still half-hoping for some miracle. Foreign radio stations such as Radio Free Europe in Munich, encouraged the Hungarians to fight on; they were full of enthusiasm for our revolution. The B.B.C. was more moderate; it gave accurage news coverage, and said that in the U. N., the General Assembly had been convened. This did not mean much but we felt that the West should accept this opportunity and sentd help.

The fighting continued, and no foreign help came. I was in one of the houses where the freedom fighters returned with their wounded, the first harbingers of yet another Hungarian tragedy. Then we knew that we were alone in our fight. The free world looked the other way.

When it was clear that the revolt was about to be crushed, more friends told me that I would be in danger. Following my years of imprisonment in Russia, I would be accused of participating in the rising. I must escape to the West. I hesitated at first, refusing to leave my family and the home to which I had only just returned. But they knew Hungary better than I did. They persisted. I sent a message to my wife, begging her to come with me and to bring our children, explaining my reasons. But she felt she could not.

Russian troops were now invading the country from Czechoslovakia, occupying the entire Austrian frontier region. We believed it would be useless to try to escape in that direction. We then heard on the radio that new groups of refugees were daily crossing the Austrian frontier and sending back radio messages from Vienna that they had safely arrived.

I left with a couple of friends and in two days, hiding from the Russian tanks, we reached Kapuvar on Lake Ferto. The local guides knew the most appropriate crossing points into Austria and were travelling to and fro day and night, with refugees. Three farmers, assisted by Hungarian frontier guides, took us to a bridge over the canal which divides the two nations; but when we arrived, we found that it had been blown up. Exhausted, we waded into Austria.

The Austrian frontier guards received us hospitably, gave us food and drink, and took us to a village where the school had been turned into a reception centre. It was equipped with a kitchen and dormitories. No one should ever forget the kindness of the Austrian people. I telephoned my relations in Vienna, who were amazed, but deeply moved, to learn that I had come alive out of that Russian hell on earth.

After only two hours in this friendly little village, my relations arrived by car and took me to Vienna where I stayed with my sister-in-law, Baroness Herbert Reichlin-Meldegg. I slept for two whole days.

I then went to my previous employers, the British Embassy in Vienna. I told them that I had worked for them in 1947; that for this I had been arrested and sentenced by the Russians to twenty-five years' hard labour as a British spy; and that during all these years of imprisonment, I had prayed to God that I might return alive and see them again.

They eyed me suspiciously, for none of them had been there in 1947. They exchanged glances and then one of them reported to his superior that a strange Hungarian, who said he had been imprisoned in Russia as a British spy, had arrived from Budapest, asking for British support. An older man came out and looked at me curiously. I told him what had happened; he seemed to believe me, for he asked me to wait while he telephoned London.

Forty-five minutes later, he returned and said that everything I had related had been confirmed. I could leave for London on the next refugee transport. I did not even have time to take leave of my relations in Vienna, because the following dawn, I was on an aircraft bound for London, with the first group of Hungarians to escape, forty-seven of us. I was still wearing my Russian prison uniform when I landed at Blackbushe.

THE END

APPENDIX

THE DEATH SENTENCE IN RUSSIA

Severe as my sentence to twenty-five years' hard labour was, I was lucky to have it passed in 1948. In any other year, I would have been executed for my alleged "high treason and espionage." "Crimes against the State" had been capital offences in Communist law from 1919 to 1947. Then, in that year, not long before my trial, capital punishment was abolished. This lasted only a little over a year, until 1949, so that my case coincided with the period of "clemency".

The reason for this, I later discovered, was that the Russian Communists, having just won a war, felt secure, and wished to show the rest of the world, where capital punishment still existed, particularly the Western democracies of Britain and America, how much more "humane" they were. Capital punishment has always been repugnant to the Slav mentality. I was to learn that if an execution had to take place it did so without the hideous Western panoply of gallows, hangman, guillotine and electric chair. The Russians preferred to send those condemned into the wood with a posse of soldiers, one of whom shot him in the head from behind when he was not expecting it.

I must support my theory about the attitude of the Russians towards capital punishment: if it has existed for political and state crimes, it never existed for civil crimes. It was introduced for these for the first time in 1961. The most sanguinary murders in our camp were punished with only a few months' imprisonment.

Why then was capital punishment for "Crimes against the State" restored in 1949, shortly after my condemnation? The reason I believe is, that by 1947, the Russians felt so secure against Western espionage that they were not frightened of it. The Western Allies had not wanted to offend their ally immediately after the war, while relations were good, and they had undertaken no espionage in Russia. Then in 1948 came the Berlin blockade and the beginning of the cold war. The Western powers found Russian espionage increasing so much in their own countries, that they had to resort to it themselves. The Soviet occupied countries soon found an increasing number of Western agents, hence their suspicion of me, and finally reintroduced the extreme penalty, to discourage them. As far as I know, the death penalty for these crimes still exists in Soviet Russia; but as soon as the leadership feels secure, I am sure they will again abolish it.

EPILOGUE

I arrived in England at an age when most men would have a settled way of life. I was filled with sadness, having been forced to abandon everything dear to me, especially my wife Maria and our two little daughters, and my beloved country. I am optimistic by nature, so there was a certain eagerness and sense of adventure now that I was rid of my communist tormentors and free to persue a new life. For a time I was accepted with kindness, and was wined and dined; but I was not offered a job, which is what I needed most. Mentally and physically, I was sick and even the clothes I wore weren't mine. I literally possessed nothing and could only communicate in basic English. To satisfy my hunger, I cleaned and painted boats in Putney; swept the Piccadilly line tube station and even organised sweepers, who were refugees like myself, to clean up more efficiently, but I was dismissed from this as the native sweepers had become uneasy that they might lose their jobs. A Hungarian friend then located a position as a doorman at the Westbury Hotel. I went for an interview but would not be accepted without recommendation. My friend Lajos Lederer, a reporter with the *Observer*, was angry about this and wrote the Hotel a letter asking "What is the world coming to when a Rupert is forced to get a recommendation to be a doorman?" I was quite happy when they hired me! I was able to eat well but I had to wear a uniform, with which I was unhappy; it had obviously been worn by many before me and looked ornate, like that which a Soviet field-marshall might wear on parade. I was not very good at the job and, much as I rushed to open taxi doors for visitors and hauled heavy luggage up to bedrooms, I somehow never managed to be at the right place when "tips" were being given; the head commissionaire always seemed to just get ahead of me!

During this period in London, I was lodging in a house belonging to a Hungarian and was grateful to have a roof over my head. However, when it came to Christmas Eve, the family's children were due home on holidays and so I was politely asked if I could go to some friends for the Christmas period. I said "of course I could" but in reality I had no friends on whom I could foist myself at this festive time. So I went to the Brompton Oratory, a nearby church, and hid behind a pillar. When the church was closed for the night, I stretched out on one of the pews and fell asleep wondering about this cold world in which I had found myself. The following morning, a considerate priest discovered me and fed me. Thus I spent my first Christmas in this free world.

My break came when I was given a job as a storeman in a textile factory. My boss was Fritzi Strasser, a Hungarian who had left Hungary many years previously and who had somehow heard of my endeavours on behalf of Jews in Hungary. He had very kindly offered me a job in his office, but I asked rather to start in the store, so that I could learn everything from the beginning. It was hard work but at last I was beginning to earn a little money; most of which went to buy medicine for my dear father, who was old and ill in Hungary. During this time, I was often summoned to Scotland Yard's special branch office and was later interrogated at great length about my past activities by MI 5. I presumed that they were trying to establish whether I had been brain-washed in the prison camps. Having helped many British people in Hungary in a humanitarian way, I was surprised and dismayed at the haughty and sometimes hostile attitude shown by my interrogators.

In 1960, Fritzi Strasser decided to set up a textile factory in Ireland's Shannon Free Zone. He sent me over to organise it, but I was not too happy about this, as I knew little about the textile business; however, I had been a legal consultant in my past, and Fritzi thought that my training in law would be useful. I set off for Ireland full of apprehension but from the moment I stepped off the aircraft at Shannon, I felt that somehow my life was going to be greatly altered for the better.

Everybody at Shannon was very friendly and welcoming. One day, as I was accompanying a colleague to the diningroom, I noticed a young girl standing at the tourist desk. As we passed, she gave me a warm smile. I was a little nonplussed, as I asumed that she had mistaken me for someone else. What I didn't know was that she was an off-duty tourist official who was trained to smile at everyone! Annie Clancy was to become my beloved wife and partner. We have been happily together for thirty years and have three children. Electronic technician Rudy lives in Heidelburg with his American wife Kathy and their two small daughters; our second son Paul, who trained as an architectural technician, has made his home at Dallas, Texas; and our daughter Anne, who married her childhood sweetheart Lloyd Nolan, happily lives near us with their little son David.

My life in Ireland has had its ups and downs. I have been disappointed with a number of people in whom I had trusted, but I have dear friends and neighbours whom I love very much. As a result, I suppose, of the unusual circumstances in which I have lived, my health has suffered. I am now confined to a wheel chair as I have lost both my legs. I always loved to ride horses and to pursue outdoor activities, so it is not easy for me to sit in a wheelchair all day and it makes me depressed at times. But my dear wife Anne keeps me optimistic; without her, I could not imagine my life.

    I had the good fortune, in June 1990, to be able to return to Hungary. The Communist regimes were crumbling, the tide was turning and it was with great satisfaction that I realised that what my father and I had suffered for, the overthrow of communism, was coming about. Our reception in my homeland was overwhelming. All my family were at the airport to greet us; my daughters and my grandchildren with whom, of course, I had kept in touch were there. Many cousins I only remembered as young children were now grey haired men; it was all very emotional. Anne and I spent the first week in Budapest where we were driven around by our son Rudy who had come from Germany to be with us; he felt himself to be a true son of Hungary. We visited friends and places, but many of the former had died which was of great sadness to me. We went to our old villa at Balaton Almádi, which is still owned by the family; I slept in the same room which I occupied as a small boy and could almost hear again my mother's voice singing a sweet, sad song. All the branches of the Rupert family reside in an area of Veszprém about ten kilometers from Almádi, where our old house still stands. Even though it is now occupied by strangers and is showing forty years of neglect, it is still known as the Rupert House. I visited my old school on the Castle Hill and was happy to see that already some priests were being allowed back to live in the Canon's Quarters of the Bishop's Palace.

At Vác, where my dear Maria lives with her sister Timmy, we had a very emotional and happy reunion and Anne was accepted as one of the family. Throughout the years, I had kept contact with my family in Hungary, so we knew each other's feelings and thoughts. I am now in my eighty-second year and I thank God to have lived to see the recent changes for good in the world; all in all, I am a very happy man

Some Books by
BALLINAKELLA PRESS

Máire Rua, *Lady of Leamaneh* - Máire MacNeill

Murrough the Burner - Ivar O'Brien

Ireland - a Thousand Kings - Hugh W. L. Weir

Upper Lough Erne in *1739* - Rev. William Henry

These My Friends & Forebears
Grania R. O'Brien

Houses of Clare - Hugh Weir

Trapa - a story in Spanish & English
Hugh Weir, Tomás Porcell

Ireland, Sketches of Some Southern Counties
George Holmes